I0155473

All Scripture references taken from the KJV of the Holy
Bible, unless otherwise indicated.

***The Christ* of GOD: Volume I** by Dr. Marlene Miles

Freshwater Press 2025

Freshwaterpress9@gmail.com

ISBN: 978-1-967860-94-4

Paperback Version

The *Christ* of *God* —God the Son

Luke 9:20 KJV

Table of Contents

This book, <u>The Christ of GOD</u> is Volume I of a three-volume series. The images on any of the covers of this series are representative only. They are not to be inferred as images of Jesus Christ and are for teaching purposes only. Neither are these images to be worshipped.

Dr. Marlene Miles

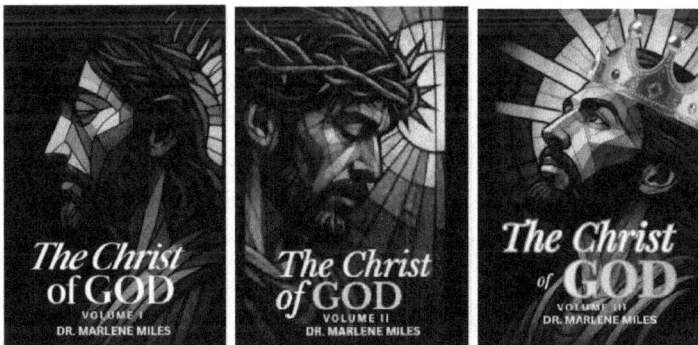

THE CHRIST of GOD

VOLUME I

INTRODUCTION

The Christ Who Seeks What Is Broken

Jesus never entered a place that was working as God intended. Jesus, The Christ of God appears only where things are not running smoothly, where things are corrupt, or failing. Brokenness of places and systems, especially spiritual systems do not present obstacles for Him; those places are His territory. This 3-book series: **The Christ of GOD** reveals Jesus through His confrontations. The Lion, the Strategist, the Disruptor. He enters every scene with purpose, brilliance, and timing. Everywhere is not because those are holy places, but because they are broken. He goes to He goes to the Temple, the synagogues, Samaria, Nazareth, Bethesda, We will explore those places more in Volume II. In this volume He finds Hagar, He confronts Joshua, He has communion with Abraham. He goes where things need to be reordered, reclaimed, fixed.

Christ walked into dark, corrupt, evil and broken places. Jesus did not come to applaud working systems. He did not come to applaud those who thought *they had it going on*, such as the Pharisees. This could be one of the reasons they wouldn't believe He was Christ. If this was the Christ, then why weren't **they** being celebrated as they thought they should? Didn't we see that same problem in Haman in the Book of Esther (6:6)

> When Haman entered, the king asked him, "What should be done for the man the king delights to honor?" Now Haman thought to himself, "Who is there that the king would rather honor than me?" (Esther 6:6 NIV)

Jesus went to those places because nothing was working. Every step He took, every village He entered, every synagogue He visited, every room, table, city, and shoreline—, there something was wrong. So, when nothing is working in your life, especially when you've tried everything – Jesus won't ignore you. It's like He likes to solve problems and puzzles. He will locate you. He will find you. Raise your hand and your voice and call on Him. Especially if your heart is broken, He will run to you.

If something needed Truth, if something needed Light or Fire, there was Jesus. Where the religious system choked people, Jesus went there. Where fear ruled, Jesus went there. Where the oppressed were silent, Jesus went there. Where people had been told "God won't show up here," Jesus arrived without hesitation.

He did not choose peaceful territory. Jesus didn't come to Earth to sightsee or to vacation. He left Glory, and by definition everything must be working correctly in Glory, or it wouldn't *be* Glory. He had a mission. He chose strategic battlegrounds. The Temple had been corrupted. The synagogues had hard-hearted people, even the teachers. Galilee was oppressed. Samaritans were confused. Nazareth was hostile toward Him, but He was raised there. Capernaum was full of privileged and yet unbelieving folks. Bethesda was spiritually broken. Creation itself--, God's own Creation was groaning under Curse. And even His Disciples were conflicted, afraid, and unprepared. This is the pattern of His ministry: Jesus goes where things are wrong to set them right.

Why?

Yes, it was His mission, but also because He came to seek and save sin sick man, and to Glorify the Father. Order does not reveal Him; brokenness does. Where religion had collapsed into ritual, He brought revelation. Where tradition suffocated Truth; He breathed life. Where leaders protected the system more than the people, He exposed them. Where oppression crushed the poor, He pushed back darkness without flinching. Where they thought the power was in the rules, He showed the power was in the One who wrote them.

This is the Christ of God: The Strategist. The Lion. The Fire. The Wisdom of God wrapped in flesh. Bold, precise, fearless. He does not avoid confrontation, He chooses it, triggers it, and uses it to reveal the Kingdom.

This book is not about the gentle Christ of paintings. This is the Christ who walks into the battlefield of human failure and turns the tide with a simple, yet profound act or a Word.

This is the Christ who outsmarts every enemy, who never panics, conveys Himself away when He should, but He never retreats. He never explains Himself, and never loses. This is the Christ who sees what's broken and says, *"I'll take that."*

He enters corruption to cleanse it. He enters confusion to correct it. He enters rejection to redefine it. He enters storms to silence them. He enters death to defeat it.

He goes where He is needed and reveals who He is. Now let us learn more about Him and then we will follow Him into each broken place and watch the Christ of God turn the world right-side up.

BEFORE THE MANGER

The Christ of God: Alpha, Origin, Eternal Son

Before He ever walked dusty roads, before He ever touched lepers or overturned tables, before Bethlehem, before Gabriel, before shepherds saw angels split the night sky, Christ already **_was_**.

Christ has to be in the beginning and at the end. He must be in Genesis and in Revelation. He is the First and the Last, Alpha and Omega. He was, is, and is to come.

There is a Hebrew narrative pattern, and it is the shape of Christ Himself.

A — Christ in Eternity (Pre-Existence)

B — Christ in Creation
C — Christ in the Old Testament
D — Christ Incarnate (on Earth)
C' — Christ in Death, Hell, Resurrection
B' — Christ in New Creation
A' — Christ in Eternity (Final Reign)

> I am the First and the Last,
> the Alpha and the Omega,
> He who was, and is, and is to come.

Therefore, Christ MUST be in this book and in this series. He must be at the beginning of Volume I; and He is. He is also at the center of Volume II. And, you will find Him at the conclusion of Volume III. This entire 3-volume work forms a Christological arc. It is chiastic. The chiastic master structure shows Christ at the Beginning and the End of Every Volume. Volume I — ALPHA (He **_Was_**). Christ before Time (Alpha). Christ in Pre-Existence, from the Intro and in every chapter and volume.

Christ is in Creation; He said, **"I, Wisdom was there."** Christ is the Word, the Logos, *in the Beginning* is Christ in the Old Testament.

We will discuss four pre-incarnate appearances of Christ in Scripture. We have already begun to discuss why Christ came to Earth, the very necessity of His incarnation.

This book begins where Scripture truly begins, not in a manger, but in Eternity. Christ of Eternity, King of Glory came to Earth enrobed in flesh to become Jesus of Nazareth. He entered history at a specific moment, but the Christ of God, the Eternal Son, has no beginning. He was not created. He is not an idea. He is not a concept that "became real" when He was born.

He is the Alpha before Creation, the Wisdom who stood beside God, the Word by whom all things were made, the Light that darkness cannot extinguish, the One who walked with Adam, the Captain of the LORD's Armies, the Fire in the furnace, the Son of Man in Daniel's vision, the Ancient Glory revealed before time began. Bethlehem is not the start of His story. Bethlehem is the moment He stepped into ours.

Christ is the First and the Last. Christ is truly the Alpha and Omega, the Beginning and the End, the One who was, and is, and is to come. He is before all things, and in Him all things hold together, and He is Lord of Eternity. Without understanding who He was before He came to Earth, we cannot fully understand who He was on Earth, nor who He is in Eternity.

Christ is not a New Testament invention. He did not begin at Christmas. He appears throughout Scripture long before Mary conceived. He was standing in the fire with Shadrach, Meshach, and Abednego. He wrestled with Jacob. He dined with Abram as Melchizedek. He confronted Joshua with a drawn sword. We see Him receiving dominion from the Ancient of

Days, forming man from the dust, and even before that, speaking galaxies into motion.

You are about to encounter the Christ the way Heaven knows Him as not merely the suffering servant but Christ, the Eternal Son. Not only the Lamb of God but the Wisdom of God. Not only the Teacher, but the Architect of the Universe. Not only the man who died, but the God who always lived.

The purpose of Volume I is to reveal the Christ of God in His pre-incarnate Glory, purpose, and power. Before the Gospels. Before the stable. Before the Cross. This is Christ in creation, in Eternity, in Divine Council, in the Old Testament, in mystery and majesty, in His eternal identity. You will see Him where you didn't expect Him. You will recognize Him where tradition rarely teaches Him. You will understand Him with deeper clarity and greater awe. The foundation of all Christian faith is not simply what Christ did, but who Christ is, Volume I unveils that foundation.

A journey in three movements. This three-volume series is intentionally structured as a chiastic arc, mirroring the Alpha and Omega nature of Christ. Volume I — He *Was* (Alpha). Christ before the manger. Volume II — He *Is* (Center). Christ on Earth. Volume III — He *Is to Come* (Omega). Christ in Glory, dominion, judgment, and Eternity. This series is no mere biography; it is a Christological epic.

And so we begin at the only true beginning: In the beginning was the Word... and the Word was with God. and the Word *was* God. Welcome to Volume I. Welcome to the Christ before time. Welcome to the Christ of God.

In the beginning was the Word, and the Word was with God, and the Word was God. The same was in the beginning with God. All things were made by him; and without him was not any thing made that was made. In him was life; and the life was the light of men. (John 1:1-3)

CHRIST, THE ANOINTED ONE

How God **anointed** Jesus of Nazareth with the Holy Ghost and with power: who went about doing good, and healing all that were oppressed of the devil; for God was with him. (Acts 10:38)

Christ means *anointed, or anointed one. Anointed*, the Greek translation of the Hebrew word rendered *Messiah.* It is not Jesus' name or last name. It is His official title. He occupies a position, an **Office** and it is named, **Christ**. It is used 514 times in the New Testament. It denotes that He was anointed or consecrated to His work as Prophet, Priest, and King of His people. He is Our Redeemer. He is Jesus the Christ (Acts 17:3, 18:5; Matthew 22:42), the Anointed One that was spoken of by Isaiah (61:1). Daniel (9:24-26), styles Him "Messiah the Prince."

He is the seed of the woman; the seed of Abraham(Genesis 22:18). He is the "Prophet like unto Moses" (Deuteronomy 18:15). He is the priest after the order of Melchizedek" (Psalm 110:4). He is the Rod Out of the Stem of Jesse" (Isaiah 11:1, 10). He is Immanuel, God With Us. He is called The Virgin's Son (Isaiah 7:14). We see Him as The Branch of Jehovah in Isaiah 4:2. And He is called by many more names, but we will see Him in these volumes as **The Christ of God**.

The Old Testament is full of prophetic declarations regarding the Great Deliverer--, Jesus the Christ, the Savior of Men. By the New Testament He has come to fulfill all in all. He has come to fulfill every prophecy. Many scholars say more than 300 prophecies. And, Amen.

ANOINTED of GOD

The Prophet Samuel anointed Saul. He also anointed David.

The Christ of God was anointed by God long before He came to Earth incarnate, long before the New Testament of the Holy Bible. Anointed of God, and on the scene from the Beginning, we can see Him throughout the Old Testament.

The kings of the earth set themselves, and the rulers take counsel together, against the LORD, and against his anointed, *saying,* (Psalm 2:2)

Real anointing comes from God. One cannot assign and anoint oneself. Man can anoint another man, but only at God's guidance and instruction. Ordained of God and by the peoples' demand for a king, Saul was anointed by Samuel, (1 Samuel 10:1). David was anointed also by Samuel (1 Samuel 16:13). When David became king of the United Kingdom of Israel the Elders of both Judah and Israel endorsed him, (2 Samuel 2:4, 2 Samuel 5:3). Solomon was anointed by Zadok the priest (with Nathan the prophet present, (1 Kings 1:39, 1:45.)

Joash (Jehoash was anointed by Jehoiada the priest (2 Kings 11:12; 2 Chronicles 23:11). The preceding anointings were God-ordained and public.

Judah

Some other kings have no record of their anointing: Rehoboam, Abijah (Abijam), Asa, Jehoshaphat, Azriah (Uzziah), Hezekiah, Josiah. Most Judean kings after Solomon do not have explicit anointing narratives, as they assumed the throne by hereditary succession unless crisis forced otherwise.

Northern Kingdom of Israel

Jeroboam was chosen by God and designated by the prophet Ahijah by prophetic investiture not by oil. (1 Kings 11:30–37). Jehu was anointed by a young prophet sent by Elisha, (2 Kings 9:1-6).

There was no public anointing for Baasha and other kings who took power by revolt or dynastic succession;

no anointings recorded. There is a pattern of those who were publicly called of God and anointed to have fared well in the office of king, or at least they started out well. Those who grabbed power --, not so much.

Jesus is King & Priest, so who Anointed the Priests? Glad you asked that.

Aaron, the first high priest was anointed by Moses (Exodus 28:41; 29:7; Leviticus 8:12). God also instructed Moses, later on to anoint Aaron's sons who were born into the high priest lineage, (Exodus 28:41; Leviticus 7:36; Exodus 40:15). High Priests after Aaron were anointed by other high priests. Eleazar, for example was consecrated by Moses (Numbers 20:25–28). Then, subsequent priests were anointed as part of priestly succession (Exodus 40:15).

Priests anointed priests. Prophets typically anointed kings.

The Christ of God is anointed by God, this is why He has attained to the Office of Christ. The anointing of the Christ of God, by God is legitimate and real.

The Lord is their
strength, and he *is* the saving strength of his **anointed**.
(Psalm 28:8)

Saying, Touch not mine **anointed**, and do my
prophets no harm. (Psalm 105:15)

God Guards the Offices. In the Old Testament, king, priest, and prophet are separate offices, and God polices the boundaries carefully. Those three offices point to **one future Person** who alone could hold all three; that Person is **Jesus Christ**:

- King (Son of David)

- Priest (after the order of Melchizedek)

- Prophet (like Moses)

Until Christ, **no man was allowed to combine the roles by force**. But they did it or tried it anyway. Kings *did* get in trouble — severely. Priests did not try to be king, but kings overstepped into the role of the priests.

- **Saul** was judged for disobedience and presumption. He stepped into the priest's role because of fear.

- **Uzziah** was judged for prideful usurpation. **2 Chronicles 26** tells us: Uzziah entered the temple, **burned incense** (explicitly priest-only). Priests confronted him. He refused to repent. "The Lord struck him with leprosy." (2 Chr 26:19). When a king **usurps priestly authority**, God judges it.

God the Son

Christ Jesus –He is Jesus Christ. (Romans 3:24; 8:1; 1 Corinthians 1:2, 30)

Christ Jesus Our Lord (Romans 8:38-39)

Christ Our Passover (1 Corinthians 5:7)

Christ the Lord (Luke 2:11)

Christ the Power of God (2 Corinthians 1:23-24)

Christ the Power of God, and the Wisdom of God (1 Corinthians 1:23-24)

The Chosen of God – The Christ of God

Christ Jesus Our Lord

Christ the King of Israel

Confidence of All the Ends of the Earth

Confidence of Them That Are Afar Off Upon the Sea

Consolation of Israel.

A Consuming Fire

The Great High Priest

He Who Filleth All in All

He That Liveth and Was Dead (Revelation 1:18)

> He who lives, and was dead. NKJV
> the living One; and I was dead. NASB
> The living one. I died, and behold I Am alive
> forevermore. ESV

The Prince of Life (Acts 3:15)

Author of Life (Acts 3:15, NIV)

Prince of Peace – *Sar Shalom*, The Messiah (Isaiah 9:6)

Prince of Princes, Prince of the Kingds of the Earth (Revelation 1:5)

Christ is a spiritual office not a gift. A gift is an ability. An office is an identity. A gift is something you DO. An office is something you **ARE**. Many can move in a spiritual gift. Only a few are appointed to a spiritual office.

To take His name in vain as in profanity but it is not limited to swearing only. It is to invoke the name "Jesus" without submission to His lordship. To take His office in vain is to use the title "Christ" while denying the authority, obedience, and cost that office requires and demands. One is personal. The other is governmental. Both are sacred.

The commandment was never only about speech. It was about bearing God's Name falsely. Israel was warned not to swear by God and disobey Him. Never claim covenant while rejecting covenant law. Never invoke authority without obedience.

CHRIST is not Jesus' last name; it is His OFFICE. "Christ" = Χριστός (Christos) = *The Anointed One*. It means the Messiah, the One sent, the One appointed, the One carrying divine authority, the One who fulfills all spiritual roles. Jesus is **The Man;** Christ is the office that He occupies eternally.

The office Christ is a prophetic office, a priestly office, a kingly office, a redemptive office, a mediatorial office, and it is an eternal office. You can't "have" Christ; you can only be Christ, and only He holds it.

This is why the demons didn't say, "We know Jesus." No, they said, "We know who You are — *the Holy One of God*." (Mark 1:24) They recognized His office before His name.

So, how do you think you are known in the spirit realm?

As another example, let's compare the office of Prophet vs. the Gift of Prophecy. With the Gift of Prophecy, anyone Spirit-filled can prophesy. It is a gift of the Spirit. It flows as the Spirit wills. It offers edification, exhortation, comfort. Having this gift may make a person "prophetic" but it does not make them a prophet. .

The Office of Prophet is different. It is assigned by God, not chosen. It carries authority, not just ability. It shapes nations, churches, leaders. It releases warnings, direction, correction. It governs spiritual atmosphere; it sets order. Those in this office will encounter spiritual opposition. It carries mantle, not just gifts. This office operates in signs and encounters and confirms destiny. It bears weight and is recognized by Heaven and hell.

A prophet is not someone who prophesies a lot. A prophet is someone who *is* a prophet.

Creation Happened Through SPEECH — and prophetic speech creates realities. God (Jesus) prophesied the world into existence. Genesis 1 repeats a rhythm: "And God SAID… and it WAS so."

God didn't think, imagine, dream, or paint Creation. He SPOKE creation. And since God is not a man that He should lie; what He spoke had to be. What He spoke came into existence. That is the essence of *prophetic function*. A prophet speaks what will be, and it becomes. But with God, the difference is that He speaks not because He sees the future. He speaks because His Word *creates* the future.

Prophecy is declaring what is not yet visible. Biblically, prophecy includes foretelling the future, revealing what is unseen, uncovering what is hidden, bringing the invisible into visibility.

Creation fits this pattern perfectly, where Things which are seen were not made of things which do appear. (Hebrews 11:3). That's a definition of prophetic creation.

God "prophesies" differently than humans. When we prophesy, we speak what the Spirit reveals. we declare what God says; we echo Heaven.

I choose to insert here that people who fake-prophesy about past things and when your birthday is, your car color, or what business you are in are not prophets; those are diviners. Well, on a good day. They could just be getting this information from Facebook. That is not prophecy. Prophets speak what is to be with a power, Grace and anointing on their spoken Word for it to come to pass – or NOT come to pass if it is a warning prophecy. God does not suffer false prophets; they didn't fare well in the Bible or in our times either.

When God speaks, reality obeys. matter forms. time arranges. light responds. laws activate. boundaries appear, dissolve or simply rearrange. So, in a very real sense Creation is God prophesying existence.

The Hebrew language confirms this

In Hebrew:

"And God said…" — *wayyōmer Elohim.* The root amar (אָמַר) is used in Scripture for decreeing, commanding, declaring, revealing, pronouncing, prophesying. God is not merely "talking." He is decreeing reality.

The New Testament agrees: Creation is prophetic speech.

In the beginning was the Word… and all things were made through Him. (John 1:1-3)

Jesus as Logos = the spoken, creative Word.

He upholds all things by the Word of His power. (Hebrews 1:3)

Creation wasn't a one-time action, the *prophetic Word* holds the universe together continuously.

The worlds were framed by the Word of God. (Hebrews 11:3)

"To frame" is architectural language. Prophetic. Creative. Constructive. When God said, 'Let there be,' He was not predicting Creation, He wasn't describing something that already existed. He was prophesying it. His Word did not describe reality; it *created* reality. The heavens and the earth are the first recorded prophecy in Scripture."

God spoke Creation the way a prophet speaks destiny — except His Word does not wait for fulfillment; it never returns void. "Creation itself is God's prophetic utterance made visible.

Just like Jesus is not Christ because He does miracles. He does miracles because He *IS* Christ.

Another example is the Office of Priest vs. Priestly Function. In the Old Testament, many Israelites made offerings. But only the priests could stand before God on behalf of others. Only the High Priest could enter behind the veil.

In the New Testament all believers have priestly access because Jesus rent the veil between mankind and God. Amen.

But Christ holds the office of High Priest

"We have a great High Priest... Jesus the Son of God." (Hebrews 4:14). This is not just a role, it is His eternal function. He intercedes. He mediates. He represents. He sanctifies. He carries blood into the Holy of Holies. He sits at the right hand as our Advocate.

No believer "steps into" the High Priest office. Christ ALONE holds it. To attempt to step into a spiritual office that is not your office is not wise and it can be very dangerous based on what opposition that particular office carries.

Offices carry **weight** — gifts carry *flow*. Think of it like this: Gifts = the RIVER, while Offices = the BANKS that shape the river. Anyone can experience flow. But only offices create structure, direction, and authority. This is why Paul writes:

He GAVE some to be Apostles... Prophets... Evangelists... Pastors... Teachers. (Ephesians 4:11) Not everyone. Some. These are offices, not gifts.

The OFFICE is the IDENTITY of that person, whereas a gift is an ability. Have you ever asked a person, or been asked, "What do you do?" That's a different question than, "Who are you, or *what* are you?" "A gift lets you function; an office lets you govern. Gifts flow; offices establish. Christ is not a role; He is the eternal office of God in flesh. Samson had the *gift* of supernatural strength. Samuel held the *office* of prophet. Aaron held the *office* of High Priest. Elijah carried a *prophetic office.* David held the *office* of king, not just the gift of leadership.

Now this is when the Christ of God really shines. Jesus fulfills all offices in one person. He is Prophet. Priest. King. Shepherd. Savior. Redeemer. Judge. Mediator. Advocate. Bridegroom. Apostle of our confession, (Hebrews 3:1). This is why His title is *Christ*.

Many can move in a gift, but only one can hold an office. Jesus didn't perform 'Christ'; He _**is**_ Christ.

If Jesus were a bagel, He would absolutely, unapologetically, gloriously be The Everything Bagel. Nothing missing; nothing broken. Why?

Because He isn't *one* office; He's **ALL** offices. He fulfills all in all. He isn't *one* role, He embodies EVERY divine role, He fulfills all in all. He isn't *one* revelation; He is ALL revelation. Fulfilling all in all. He isn't *one* attribute; He carries the FULLNESS of the Godhead bodily. The Christ of God is everything.

No one else in Scripture "stacks" roles like that.

Everyone else is a type, a shadow, a glimpse, a foretaste, a partial picture.

But Jesus "Christ is the Everything Bagel of Heaven. He is *all that*. He is every office, every anointing, every function of God's authority baked into one Person.

ONE OR A FEW

Pre-Incarnate Christ Spoke to One or a Few at a Time

In the Old Testament "Christ appearances" are always to individuals or very small groups. Despise not small beginnings. If you find yourself talking with or ministering to one or a few it could be that is who you are called to. Or, it could be because you are *becoming* but you have not been fully revealed yet. So, there is the Old Testament Christ and then there is the New Testament

Jesus Christ. These pre-incarnate appearances (The Angel of the LORD / The LORD in bodily form) are *always personal*, intimate, and direct.

Adam & Eve - God came down and walked with them in the cool of the day. At first that was good, but then things went awry and something needed fixing.

Hagar (alone in the wilderness, with her son, Ishmael. (Genesis 16). He meets ONE broken woman.

Abraham (alone or with a small household) (Genesis 18.) He appears to ONE man under the oaks of Mamre.

Jacob (alone at the river), (Genesis 32) He wrestles with ONE man till daybreak.

Moses alone at the burning bush, (Exodus 3) He calls ONE man.

Joshua (alone near Jericho), (Joshua 5) The Captain of the LORD's Army appears to ONE leader.

Manoah and his wife (Samson's parents), (Judges 13). A couple — not a crowd.

Isaiah's throne-room vision, (Isaiah 6). One prophet sees Him.

Daniel's vision of the "Son of Man" (Daniel 7). One prophet sees Him in glory.

Never once does the Old Testament show the pre-incarnate Christ speaking to a *crowd, nation, multitude,* or *assembly*. Always one person, or at most a couple. This is consistent and intentional.

The New Testament Jesus appears publicly, openly, and to multitudes. After the Incarnation, everything changes. Christ is no longer hidden, selective, or appearing to **chosen** vessels only. Now, He appears to the world. At the Sermon on the Mount, thousands gathered (Matthew 5–7).

Feeding 5,000 - A massive crowd (John 6). He was teaching by the Sea, crowds pressed Him (Luke 5). He healed all who came, even multitudes, (Matthew 12:15).

Triumphal Entry- the entire city was moved to worship (Matthew 21). After the Resurrection, *"He appeared to more than 500 at once"* (1 Corinthians 15:6)

This is a dramatic shift. *But why?*

In the Old Testament: Christ is revealed privately. Because redemption is not yet accomplished. He appears to patriarchs, prophets, covenant carriers, intercessors, judges, leaders, forerunners. These are *seed carriers* of His story.

In the New Testament: Christ is revealed publicly because redemption has come. He now appears to crowds, villages, cities, nations, the poor, rich, sick, oppressed, even to multitudes without number, because the Messiah has moved from hidden revelation to public proclamation.

Old Testament Christ was revealed to individuals. New Testament Christ is revealed to multitudes. In the Old Testament He met one man; in the New Testament He met mankind.

This reinforces His eternal identity and His unfolding revelation throughout history. Old Testament Christ appears selectively. New Testament Christ appears universally. Because the Incarnation changes access. Christ moves from shadow to substance, From private, to public. He moves from hidden, to revealed. From foretelling, to fulfilling. Jesus moves in His assignment in boldness. He moves in His mission to confrontation. He moves into being revealed as He enters public ministry.

Jesus is never shown dealing with multitudes anywhere in the Old Testament, only individuals or one or a few at a time.

Jesus is all Spirit. Spirits need a body in the Earth. Just as we say, "Lord, clothe me in the right garment to go through a certain gate or to be in the presence of God," we are talking about certain spiritual realms. In the Earth realm, the human "robe" the human garment is needed to walk and transact business here. In spiritual realms, we need a different "robe." Additionally, *spirits* are invisible except to those with "spiritual vision," therefore, even if Jesus sat on a bench in the park, 24/7, almost no one would "see" Him there. But as a man, when Jesus is here on Earth, everyone or at least multitudes of people can see Him.

Old Testament Christ appeared to certain select individuals--, those who were **chosen**. New Testament Christ appeared to multitudes, those *called* to seek and follow Him. This is a Biblical pattern, not a coincidence. In the Old Testament, Christ appears only to a handful of **chosen** individuals such as: Abraham, Jacob, Moses, Joshua, Gideon, Samson's parents, Isaiah, Daniel. These were not just *"called."* These were chosen vessels, handpicked for specific assignments, covenants, and divine transitions. He revealed Himself to the chosen., not the many.

This matches the principle, "Few are chosen."

New Testament: Multitudes represent those who are *called.* Then suddenly, once Christ comes in the flesh, He teaches multitudes. He heals multitudes. He feeds multitudes. He moves among towns and cities. He proclaims the Kingdom publicly. For the first time, Christ allows Himself to be accessible to the many, which are the *"called."*

Too many teachers, preachers and so on believe they are called to multitudes. *Are they?* Perhaps they are only called to select few, which are the chosen. But the ambitious seek out the multitudes and then believe they will find the **chosen** in that great gathering. Some behave as if they are the only chosen, the last chosen, and no one else is or will ever be chosen again. They behave as if all those in the multitudes are their subjects. This is not of God, and it is not His way.

I'm judging no one; only God knows.

Jesus' ministry becomes public, broad, open, universal, multitudinous. This matches the other half of the principle "Many are *called*." The many that are called are called to God, through Jesus Christ. That is God's way.

The revelation is that the incarnation opens the calling. Before the incarnation, access to God was very restricted. Revelation was selective. Appearances were strategic. Encounters were prophetic assignments. Christ appears only to those who were chosen because redemption had not yet been revealed.

After the Incarnation, the veil is torn, access is universal; healing is for all. The Gospel is preached to every creature. Now all are *called*, but only those who respond become **chosen**. This is why Jesus says,

> "If any man will come after Me…"
> (Matthew 16:24)

and

> "Whosoever will, let him come…"
> (Revelation 22:17)

Put simply, in the Old Testament there were a chosen few. In the New Testament many were called into the Kingdom. From the many called, chosen ones were selected. Christ first meets individuals. Then He meets the world. Then He calls His Disciples from the crowd. Then He commissions them to call others. Then He chooses again from those who respond.

In the Old Testament, Christ came to the **chosen**. In the New Testament, He came to the *called*. And in the Kingdom, He chooses again from among the *called*. He revealed Himself to the few before He revealed Himself to the many, so that the **chosen** could prepare the way for the *called*.

CALLED AND CHOSEN

The Pattern Of His Appearing

There is a rhythm to the revelation of Christ across Scripture. A divine sequence. A pattern that holds the whole story together. In the Old Testament, Christ appears to the **chosen**. In the New Testament, He appears to the *called*. And in the Kingdom, He chooses again from among the *called*. This is not poetic license; this is Biblical architecture.

Before Bethlehem, Christ was revealed only to the **chosen**. All throughout the Old Testament, when the pre-incarnate Christ appears, He comes to *individuals*. Abraham under the oaks. Jacob at the river. Moses at the bush. Joshua near Jericho. Gideon in the winepress. Manoah and his wife. Isaiah in the temple. Daniel in visions

Never once in the Old Testament does He call a *crowd*. He does not speak to *cities*. He does not teach the *masses*. He does not gather *multitudes*.

His revelation is private, precise, and prophetic. He appears to those who carry covenant, lineage, assignment, and destiny. People we call "patriarchs" or "prophets" today were, in their own time, the chosen few — recipients of divine visitation not because they were perfect, but because they were *appointed*.

Christ appears to them because They are carriers of promise. They are bridges between dispensations. They are pivots in the story. They bear the weight of transition. Through them the Christ-line is preserved. This is the domain of the **chosen**. Few see Him. Few hear Him. Few encounter Him. Because the Redemption has not yet been revealed to the world.

Hidden Glory is for chosen witnesses.

After Bethlehem, Christ is revealed to the multitudes. Once Christ enters the world in flesh, everything changes. He steps into the public square. For the first time in history, entire villages gather. Entire cities come out.

Throngs press Him. Waves of people follow Him. multitudes sit to hear Him. The world is invited to see Him.

He feeds 5,000. He feeds 4,000. He heals *everyone* who touches Him. He teaches from boats because the crowds are too large. He speaks on mountainsides because no building can contain them. Suddenly Christ is public, not private. The *called* come running. This is the shift from *selective revelation* to universal invitation. Here, we begin to see **chosen** *witnesses out of called multitudes. We see isolated encounters now have become open proclamation.* The Incarnation opens the gates of access.

Where the Old Testament whispered **chosen**, the New Testament declares "whosoever will."

Many are now *called*.

Now, select ones are chosen from among the called but the pattern does not end in the Gospels. Once the multitudes are *called*, Christ begins choosing again. From the many, He selects twelve. From the twelve, He chooses three. From the crowds, He calls disciples. From the disciples, He appoints apostles. From the apostles, He commissions witnesses. This is the divine sequence. There is the call. The people respond. Jesus chooses and equips and then sends. He is always calling the world, but He is always choosing from among the responders. Because calling is universal, but choosing is purposeful.

The Kingdom is not only populated by the *called,* it is led, moved, carried, and advanced by the **chosen**. As Jesus Himself said,

"You have not chosen Me, but I have chosen you and ordained you." (John 15:16)

The pattern remains intact.

This progression reveals something profound about the nature of Jesus. He is the same Christ in every era, but the access to Him changes with the covenant.

Old Covenant Christ preserved revelation for chosen vessels who carried the lineage and message. New Covenant Christ broadcasts revelation so the whole world may see and hear.

Kingdom Age Christ selects laborers, disciples, sons, and servants from among the *called*, those whose hearts respond to Him.

The Christ of the Old Testament is no different from the Christ of the Gospels; it is the *administration* of revelation that changes. He was veiled for the **chosen**. He was revealed for the *called*. And He anoints the **chosen** who answer His call.

In the Old Testament, Christ came to the **chosen**. In the New Testament, He came to the *called*. And in the Kingdom, He chooses again from among the **called**. And the mystery becomes clear. God did not change. Christ did not change. The Spirit did not change. But access did.

Revelation grows from individual to the multitude, to the remnant, to Glory. This is the story of Christ unfolding in three acts: from Abraham to Bethlehem, from Bethlehem to Pentecost, from Pentecost to the Kingdom.

E PLURIBUS UNUM

From Many, One

E pluribus unum is Latin. It means, *"out of many, one."* It was originally used to describe thirteen U.S. colonies becoming one nation, but the phrase is spiritually accurate and applicable. The *called* are many. The **chosen** is one. The *called* are The many, and The **chosen** is The "One. This mirrors the Biblical pattern where God calls many, but He chooses one for a particular assignment. From many voices, the Lord raises one voice. From many disciples, does He not send one apostle? From many nations, He forms one kingdom. From many members, He builds one Body. From many believers, He unites one Bride. From many seeds, He grows one harvest.

He is God. He is the Lord.

This is the rhythm of divine selection. In the Old Testament, Christ came to the chosen. In the New Testament, He came to the *called*. And in the Kingdom, He chooses again from among the *called*. That's literally *e pluribus unum,* spiritually speaking.

God calls the *multitude*, and from that multitude He draws a *remnant,* a people formed into one purpose.

There are Scriptural patterns that match *e pluribus unum*. Israel itself. Out of many nations there was one **chosen** nation. The Disciples were chosen out of many followers. At first 12 were chosen. Out of the twelve, three were drawn near. Out of the three, one given Revelation. Many to few, to one.

And then there's the Church. Out of all the Earth one Body, the Body of Christ. Out of many members, the Lord will unite and select His one Bride. In Salvation, many are *called* by the Gospel, and one is led to become a new creation in Christ. The Kingdom follows a divine *e pluribus unum* pattern. Many are called, but out of the many, God forms one people, one witness, one Body, one Bride.

If you think of this in your own family, your family is one bloodline, but there are many people and may be multiple families in that bloodline. When God looks at you, He sees one individual, but He also sees your family and beyond that, your one bloodline. Pray for your bloodlines as well as you pray for yourself and your family.

Out of the *called* (the many), Christ draws the **chosen** (the one). This is Heaven's *e pluribus unum*.

Hear O Israel, the Lord Our God is one, Amen.
(Deuteronomy 6:4)

THE MYSTERY OF THIRTEEN

The Called & the Chosen

There is a thread running through Scripture from Genesis to Revelation. It's like a golden thread woven through covenants, callings, tribes, disciples, and destinies. It is the pattern of the *called* and the **chosen**, a pattern Jesus Himself summarized in one brief but explosive verse:

Many are called, but few are chosen.
(Matthew 22:14)

These words are key. They are a doorway, a diagnostic into how Christ forms His people, His leaders, His vessels, and His world. If we listen closely, the pattern becomes unmistakable.

The *called*: the many who hear His voice. Christ calls broadly. He calls openly. He calls generously. He calls cities, nations, villages, crowds, sinners, seekers, the weary, the broken, the fed-up, the curious, the resistant, the hungry, the apathetic and indifferent. He calls the sick, the lame, the halt, the blind, the deaf. He calls everyone and invites them to the Marriage Feast.

The calling is universal and without prejudice.

It spreads like seeds sowed in every direction.

It lands on good soil, hard soil, shallow soil, thorny soil, dry soil. But the calling is for everyone because God never withholds His voice. He rains on the just and the unjust alike. He is not a respecter of persons, and neither should we be. Jesus preached where everyone could hear. He fed multitudes. He healed crowds. He proclaimed the Kingdom openly.

The calling always begins with abundance. Plenty. Overflow. To all people, all nations; folks everywhere. For example, at the grocery store or the farmer's market, or the orchard itself, there may be many apples in reach. But only one apple is chosen. Maybe it's not the prettiest or the largest. Not the most polished. The one chosen by purpose.

Jesus understood that orchard truth long before we ever did. Because calling is the orchard. Choosing is the picking.

The **chosen,** the few who answer the call Christ chooses differently from how He calls. The calling is broad. The choosing is precise. He chooses Abraham, not Ur. Moses, not Egypt. Gideon, not the host of Israel. David, not his brothers. Mary, not every virgin. John the Baptist, not every priest's son. Twelve disciples, not every follower. Three inner-circle Disciples, not all twelve.

The higher the assignment, the narrower the selection is.

In the Old Testament, Christ appeared to individuals, not crowds. Because these were not just *called*—they were **chosen**. Chosen for covenant, leadership, transition, revelation, promise, destiny. They were **chosen** because through them God could weave the next chapter of redemption.

And then comes the astonishing shift. The Incarnation. This is when the *called* become or show up as the multitudes. Christ arrives in flesh. And for the first time in history, He turns His face toward the multitudes. Tribal and ethnic feuds were famous then, Jews don't talk to Samaritans and vice versa, and so on. in that time and culture people didn't even look at the sick, halt, lame, deaf, or blind. (What's changed, *right*?) Jesus dealt with all of them from publicans, tax collectors, from poor people to prostitutes and so on, teaching them. Healing them. Feeding them. Calling them. Inviting them. This is the age of calling.

All who are weary. Whosoever will. If any man thirst. Those who have no money, come and buy. If any man follow Me. To the Jew first, and also to the Greek. To every creature. To the ends of the Earth.

Many, many, many. This is the season of abundance, it is the season of the orchard in full bloom. But from the *called*, Christ begins selecting again.

The pattern of 13 emerges when one chosen leads the twelve. Christ does something that Heaven has done before. He forms a unit of 13. One chosen (Christ) leading the Twelve who are *called*, then they become **chosen**). It mirrors Moses and the 12 tribes. It mirrors Jacob and his 12 sons (13 counting Joseph/Ephraim-Manasseh). It mirrors divine structure. Christ calls many. But He chooses twelve.

From the called, He chooses leaders. From the multitude, He selects disciples. And this "13 pattern" becomes a spiritual signature:

- Many → One
- *Pluribus → Unum*
- Called → Chosen
- Crowd → Disciple
- Seed → Harvest

- Kingdom → Remnant

The phrase *e pluribus unum* echoes a Kingdom pattern. Out of the many, one is formed. Or in Christ's language, Many are *called*, but few are **chosen**.

E pluribus unum is not a coincidence; it is a Kingdom pattern. Long before it became a political motto, it was a Kingdom Truth. It describes Israel. It describes Christ and the Twelve. It describes the Church, the Body of Christ. It describes the Remnant, the Bride. Even the character of God's interactions with humanity. God sows widely and selects purposefully. He calls the world. He chooses those who answer. He scatters the seed. He picks the fruit. He calls the multitude. He chooses the disciple. He calls the entire orchard. Every tree performs, every blossom buds, every branch bears fruit. Then, He chooses the apple.

In the Old Testament, Christ came to the **chosen**. In the New Testament, He came to the *called*. And in the Kingdom, He chooses again from among the *called*. It is the divine *e pluribus unum*. Out of the many *called*, God forms and equips the one **chosen**.

Christ still calls many. He still chooses from among them. And He still plants orchards of possibility in every generation. But only those who answer the call become chosen. Only those who follow become disciples. Only those who surrender become chosen vessels.

THE HEAVENLY COUNCIL DECISION: WHO WILL GO FOR US?

The Sending of the Son Before Time Began

Before the manger, before Mary, before shepherds heard angels sing, before a star rose in the East, a divine decision was made. Not on Earth. Not in a palace. Not in a temple. Not among prophets or priests. But in Heaven's council, the eternal throne room where Father, Son, and Spirit communed in perfect unity.

The incarnation was not reaction. It was not improvisation. It was not God "trying something new." It was the execution of a decision made in eternity past.

A question echoes in the Council of Heaven. Isaiah hears Heaven's conversation "Whom shall I send, and who will go for *us*?" (Isaiah 6:8). This was not God speaking to Angels since Angels are never included in divine decision-making, They are servants, not strategists. This was Father, Son, and Spirit speaking within Themselves.

The "Us" is Trinitarian. The question is divine. The mission is eternal. Before Abraham, before Israel, before sin even entered the world, God already planned Redemption.

Revelation reveals the staggering truth "The Lamb was slain from the foundation of the world." (Revelation 13:8). This means Christ's mission was not Plan B. The Cross was not an emergency response. Redemption was not an afterthought. God knew the cost before creating humanity. Christ accepted the mission before Adam breathed. In eternity past, the Son offered Himself before the world needed saving.

This is Divine Love at its purest form. It is a sacrifice planned before the need existed.

The Son volunteers. In the Divine Council, Christ answers the eternal question, **"Here am I. Send Me."** He does not hesitate. He does not negotiate. He does not protest. He steps forward with the full knowledge of

46

betrayal, rejection, mockery, death, separation, suffering, burial, wrath, the weight of the world's sin, the agony of the Cross. He says, "**Yes**," knowing exactly what it will cost Him. He agrees to take on flesh knowing what flesh would feel.

He embraces Time knowing He has always lived outside of it. He consents to mortality knowing He is immortal. He prepares to enter the womb knowing He fills the universe. This is not duty. This is *agape* Love.

The Father sends Him, not as a messenger, but as a mission. The Father sends the Son, and He sends Him full of authority,

God so loved the world that He gave His only begotten Son. (John 3:16)

He gave Him not as an emissary, or as an Angel, or a prophet, not even as a vision but as God in flesh, the exact image of the invisible God. Christ is not merely *sent*; He is given. Christ was given to the world, given to humanity, given to suffering, death, and to the Cross. The Son was given to us.

The Spirit anoints Him before He arrives. Isaiah prophesied it.

The Spirit of the Lord is upon Me, (Isaiah 61:1)

This is speaking of Christ, prophetically before He is born.

In Heaven's Council, the Spirit is already assigned to overshadow Mary, empower the Son, manifest divine works, sustain Him in suffering, raise Him from death, empower the church, complete the mission. Father, Son, and Spirit, are in full agreement. The incarnation is a Trinitarian mission.

The Incarnation was always the plan the prophets hint at it. The Angels anticipated it. Creation groaned for it. Hell feared it. Heaven prepared for it. From Genesis to Malachi, the entire Old Testament leans forward, waiting for the moment when the Eternal Son would enter the world He created.

This chapter reveals the truth that Christ was not sent reluctantly; He was sent intentionally. He was sent eternally. He was sent in perfect unity with the Father and the Spirit. Before time began, Christ said, "**Yes**."

Human incarnation of The Christ of God is not a reaction to human failure, God changing His mind, a divine course correction, or the result of Israel's disobedience. It was the plan before humans fell, before time began, before Creation was spoken into existence.

Understanding this changes everything. It reveals Christ's eternal love, Heaven's united purpose, the cosmic significance of the Cross, the intentionality behind redemption, the depth of the Father's plan, the Son's willingness, the Spirit's empowerment. The world was out of order, so Heaven decided to send the One who could reorder everything.

This is the Christ of God before Bethlehem, before time, before the universe.

THE "NEARLYS"

The Men Who Foreshadowed Christ

Scripture introduces us to men who were almost. They were types and shadows, hints, previews of the Christ to come. Each carried a fragment of His nature, but none carried the fullness. They were lamps; He is the Light. They were images; He is the Image. They were types; He is the Truth.

The previous chapter prepares the way for the incarnation itself, but first we look at the *nearly-there's* of the Old Testament.

1. Adam — The First "Son of God" was created in God's image. He was given dominion over Creation, and He represented all humanity. **Christ came to correct that. He is the Last Adam; He is the restoration of what Adam lost.**

2. Abel — The Innocent Shepherd was a righteous man. Abel was a shepherd, and His offering pleased God. He was murdered by his own brother. Judas who was close was the one who betrayed Jesus and then He was crucified. **Christ is the Greater. Abel's blood is the innocent blood that speaks better things.**

3. Melchizedek — Priest-King of Salem was King AND Priest. Ther is no recorded beginning or end. He Gave bread and wine but only to Abraham. Even though he was pre-incarnate Christ He was not revealed and He did not draw all men unto Himself. **Christ is the true Priest-King forever after this order.**

4. Noah — The Deliverer Through Water was a righteous man. He saved a remnant. He built the ark (a type of Christ). Noah brought humanity into a new covenant. **Christ is the Ark we enter to escape judgment.**

5. Abraham — The Father of Faith left everything at God's call. Abraham believed God. He offered his "only son." He received promises that bless all nations. **Christ is the promised Seed and the ultimate sacrifice.**

6. Isaac — The Promised Son was born by miraculous birth. He was the only son of Abraham and Sarah. He carried the wood, just as Jesus carried that Cross to Golgotha. He laid down willingly, but a ram (substitute) took his place. **Christ is the true Son who completes what Isaac foreshadowed.**

7. Jacob — The Chosen Over the Stronger elder brother. Jacob was the younger chosen over the older. He wrestled with God. Jesus "wrestled" with His assignment while He was in Gethsemane. Jacob's name was changed, and he became the father of the 12 Tribes of Israel. **Christ is the one who wrestles and blesses, the true Israel.**

8. Joseph — The Suffering Exalted Savior. Joseph was a beloved son hated by his own brothers. He was sold for silver, just as Jesus was. He was wrongfully accused, just as Jesus was. He was sold into slavery. Judas sold Jesus for the price of a slave—20 pieces of silver. Joseph was eventually raised to the throne from the pit and the prison to save the whole world. **Christ is the Greater Joseph — the Savior of nations.**

9. Moses — The Deliverer and Lawgiver was delivered from death as an infant. Moses confronted a king (Pharaoh). He brought people out of bondage. He was the Mediator of covenant. He Spoke with God face to face. **Christ is the final Prophet like Moses.**

10. Joshua — The Captain of Salvation
was a type and shadow of the Christ. His name literally means "Yeshua / Jesus." Joshua led people into promised inheritance. He followed God wholeheartedly. **Christ is the One who brings us into the true Promised Land.**

11. Aaron — The High Priest
bore the names of the people. He offered sacrifices. He entered the Holy of Holies. **Christ is the perfect High Priest.**

12. David — The Warrior-King
was a shepherd. He was anointed. He was a giant-slayer. He is the King of Israel. He was a man after God's heart. He was a Covenant carrier. **Christ is the Greater David — the Eternal King.**

13. Solomon — The Man of Wisdom and Peace.
He was the son of David, as is Jesus, by lineage. He had a glorious kingdom. His Wisdom that astonished nations. **Christ is the true Wisdom of God and the Prince of Peace.**

14. Elijah — The Fire Prophet
confronted idolatry. He called down fire. He ascended into Heaven. **Christ is the one who baptizes with the Holy Spirit and Fire.**

15. Elisha — The Double-Portion Healer multiplied bread. Raised the dead. Healed lepers. Miracles flowed through him. **Christ is the source of all healing and resurrection power.**

16. Samuel — The Ear that Hears God was born by miracle. He was dedicated to God. He was the Voice of God in a corrupt generation. **Christ is the perfect Prophet who hears and speaks flawlessly.**

17. Boaz — The Kinsman-Redeemer was wealthy, kind, and he redeemed a foreign bride. **Christ is our Redeemer who marries the Gentile Bride.**

18. Jonah — The Man of Three Days. He was thrown into the deep. He was Three days "buried." Came back to preach repentance. **Christ fulfills the sign of Jonah in resurrection.**

19. Samson — The Strong Deliverer, was announced by an Angel. He was a Nazarite from birth. He fought Israel's enemies alone. He even destroyed enemies in his death. **Christ destroys the works of darkness by His death.**

20. Zerubbabel — The Builder of the Temple was anointed to rebuild. Empowered by the Spirit. Finished what he started. **Christ builds the true temple — the Church.**

IT HAD TO BE HIM

Why Christ Had to Come to Earth

To understand the incarnation, to understand the Cross, to understand the mission of Christ, you must first understand this: Earth was out of order. Humanity was out of order. The systems of the world were out of order. Even religion was out of order.

Christ did not enter a world that was functioning. He entered a world that was failing. He did not come to admire what people built. He came to restore what had collapsed. He did not come because things were good. He came because everything was broken. From Eden to Babylon to Rome, from the fall to the flood to the exile, Scripture paints one unbroken truth:

Humanity cannot fix itself. Only Christ can.

The Fall was the first shattering of order In Eden, divine order was simple: God reigns. Humanity reflects. Creation flourishes. Communion flows. But when Adam fell, the world fell with him. The Curse did not affect Adam alone. It twisted relationships, desires, identity, nature, Creation, Time, and destiny. The dominoes of disorder began falling and have never stopped. Until Christ.

By Noah's Day: violence filled the Earth

The earth was filled with violence. (Genesis 6:13)

There weren't just pockets of violence in a fallen world, not just regions, but the whole Earth. Every imagination of the human heart was evil continually. Creation was corrupted to its core.

This is why Christ later calls the days before His return "as the days of Noah." He didn't mean this as a timeline, but He was describing a condition. It was chaos. There was widespread violence, confusion, and rebellion.

Rebellion and disorder were organized at Babel. Babel. Of course, you've heard of organized crime. The dark kingdom is organized. It is violent, full of corruption, stealing, killing, and destroying. But it is organized. Back to this tower at Babel. It is not just a tower, It is the first global act of organized rebellion. Humanity united, not under God, but against Him. Their motto was, "Let us make a name for ourselves."

The world's systems were born here. All systems, whether political, religious, or ideological, and they were all built on pride. Christ would one day confront these systems directly and decisively.

Israel was the **chosen**, but she was also out of order. God chose a nation to reveal Himself to the world. But even Israel fell into idolatry, injustice, corruption, rebellion, division, spiritual blindness, prophetic silence. The priests became corrupted. The kings became oppressive. The prophets were persecuted. The temple became a marketplace. The Law became a weapon against the weak.

The very nation chosen to reflect God became a mirror of human brokenness.

Between the Book of Malachi and the Book of Matthew there were four hundred years of silence. Were they too busy sinning to do anything Godly? Had God turned them over to their own devices?

The last words of the Old Testament end with a threat: "Lest I come and strike the land with a curse." Then Heaven falls silent. No prophets. No angels. No glory. No theophanies. No fresh revelation.

Just silence.

The political world collapses into empire. The religious world fractures into sects. The spiritual world becomes dry and ritualistic. By the time Christ arrives, Rome rules with iron. Herod rules with paranoia. Pharisees rule with legalism. Sadducees rule with compromise. Zealots rule with violence. Tax collectors rule with corruption, and Satan rules through fear.

Israel is waiting for Messiah but would not recognize Him when He came. Everything is out of order.

The world needed Christ because they needed more than a moral teacher. More than a prophet. More than inspiration. More than religion. The world needed: a Second Adam, a final High Priest. a perfect King, a true Prophet, a Deliverer from darkness. a Destroyer of demonic powers. a Restorer of Creation. a Redeemer of humanity. The world needed a Rebuilder of divine order. Fortunately, Christ is all of these.

He came because the image of God was broken, the world was spiritually bankrupt, demons operated freely. religion had become corrupted. human nature had collapsed. no one could save themselves

Christ steps into history not as an observer, but as the One who restores everything to its original design. The Incarnation was Heaven's intervention into disorder. When Christ is born, Heaven interrupts the chaos of Earth.

The Incarnation is not soft. It is violent— a direct invasion against sin, sickness, darkness, lies, Death, Hell, corruption, spiritual blindness. Christ did not come to comfort disorder; He came to confront it. He came because the world was too broken to repair itself. He came because creation groaned for restoration. He came because divine order had to be reestablished— in hearts, in systems, in nations, and ultimately in the universe itself.

We all must understand how broken the world was, so by comparison we can understand how powerful Christ is. Understand how deep the disorder was, so you can grasp how necessary His mission was. Christ does not enter a functioning world, He enters a fallen one.

From my books, **Darkness and Light: *The Struggle for Your Glory*, and the** book, **Without Form: Finish the Work** we know that when God made the Heavens and the Earth that God said, "**IT IS GOOD**." But just a few verses later, darkness was over the face of the deep. (Genesis). So, what happened?

Whatever happened it needed to be corrected. Adam and Eve were put in the Garden to have stewardship over the Garden. They were supposed to be fruitful and multiply and replenish the Earth. Replenish it with what? What was there before? Where did it go? God said, Replenish the Earth.

So, it seems that Adam and Eve were supposed to step into the position of correcting things that had gone wrong after God's original Creation, but Adam and Eve failed. That's why there was so much disorder. That's why Jesus had to come to Earth at clutch times in the dispensation of the Old Testament, and then later He had to come to Earth in flesh.

He came because everything was out of order—and only He could put it back together. There were other types and shadows of Christ prior to His arrival in the manger in Bethlehem. Those were the nearly-there's that we discussed in the preceding chapter.

THE CHRIST BEFORE TIME

The Eternal Son, Not A Created Being

Every story has a beginning except Christ's. Every being has an origin except Christ. Every life enters through time except the One who created time. Before Genesis opened its first line, before the Spirit hovered over the deep, before the first atom obeyed the divine command to exist, Christ already *was*. He was not becoming, not emerging, and not forming; He **_Was_**.

This is the first revelation every believer must get a hold of, Christ does not begin in the New Testament. Christ begins in eternity.

In the Beginning *Was* the Word" — What That Actually Means John does not say *"In the beginning became the Word,"* or *"In the beginning God created the Word,"* or *"In the beginning the Word appeared."* He writes with absolute finality:

In the beginning *was* the Word. (John 1:1)

When the Beginning began, Christ was already there. When creation started, Christ was not part of it, He was the cause of it. When time started ticking, Christ was not waiting, He was already reigning. Time is the robe He wears, not the place He dwells.

Christ is Eternal Son, not eternal idea. He is not divine concept. He is not a poetic metaphor. He is not merely the "thoughts" of God made flesh. He is the Son; co-equal with the Father, co-eternal with the Spirit. He is sharing the divine essence. He is the radiant image of the invisible God--, the exact imprint of His nature.

The Son did not *become* divine; He **is** eternally divine. The Son did not have to *earn* God's approval. He has always been the Father's delight. The Son did not grow into glory. He shared Glory "before the world was." Christ **is** God's story.

The Eternal Son matters because if Christ had a beginning, then He could have an end. If Christ were created, He could be dethroned. If Christ were less than the Father, He could not save. Only the Eternal Son, The Christ of God can forgive sin, conquer death, judge angels, redeem humanity, rule the nations, and inaugurate a new creation.

Salvation is not built on a religious figure. It is built on the eternal nature of Christ.

The Son is beside the Father, not behind Him. Proverbs 8 portrays the pre-incarnate Christ as Wisdom, standing beside the Father at Creation "**Then I was beside Him, daily His delight.**" --Beside, not below, with, not after, co-working, not observing. Christ is the eternal companion of the Father, in the Divine Council of Creation.

When the Father willed, the Son spoke, and the Spirit energized. Creation is the product of the Triune harmony of Father, Son, and Spirit. This is why Christ moves through Scripture with effortless authority. He is not borrowing power. He is exercising His own.

The Son is the center of Heaven's worship. Even before the world began. Heaven's adoration did not begin at the Resurrection. It did not start with the angels in Bethlehem. Long before Earth existed, long before angels were sent, long before galaxies spun into motion, Christ was the center of Heaven's worship. He was the radiance, the beauty, the joy, the delight, the focus, the crown, the wonder, the beloved of eternity. He is the Bright and Morning Star. He was not waiting to be born. He was ruling.

Christ did not *become* "Christ" — He always was the Christ of God. Many imagine that "Christ" means "the role Jesus took on as Savior. Christ means Anointed One, the divine office belonging to the eternal Son. He was Christ before Mary and Joseph. shepherds, wise men, Bethlehem. He was Christ before He came to Earth and the Angels sang. Before prophecy manifested, He was.

He did not earn the title, *Christ*. He is Christ: The Christ of God; He is the *everything* of God. His incarnation did not **make** Him something new, it revealed, in flesh, to us, who are also in flesh, who He has always been.

If, when talking about Jesus, you start with Bethlehem, you start in the wrong place; you're backing up, as they say in the South.

Christ cannot be understood unless He is placed where He has always existed: In the Beginning, before the Beginning, and after the end. He is the First. He is the Origin. He is the Source. Everything else we study, Creation, Old Testament appearances, Incarnation, Death, Resurrection, dominion, Eternity flows from this truth. He is eternal. He is God. He is Christ. And He was here **before** all things.

THE APPOINTED TIME

Why Christ Came When He Did — and Not Earlier or Later

Christ did not arrive in a random century. He did not appear at a convenient political moment. He did not come during Israel's glory, nor in Moses' era of miracles, nor during David's kingdom of worship.

He came in the quietest, darkest, most unexpected time. A time chosen not by prophets, a time when no other prophets' voices were being heard in the Earth. He didn't come at a time chosen by Israel, not by Rome, not by human need...but by Heaven's clock. Scripture calls it "the fullness of time" in Galatians 4:4

Heaven does nothing late, nothing early, nothing accidental. Everything God does is timed to perfection.

Why not during the days of Moses? Moses opened the Red Sea. Christ could have appeared then and led Israel directly. But Christ came after the Law so He could fulfill it. He could not fulfill a covenant that did not yet exist. He waited for the Law to run its course and reveal humanity's inability to obey.

Then He came as the only One who ever could.

Why not during David's Kingdom? David's reign was glorious, the perfect moment for Messiah to sit on a throne. But Christ did not come to inherit a Kingdom. He came to establish one.

He did not come to sit on David's throne yet. He came to conquer sin, Death, and Hell first. He came to take the Cross before He takes the throne. David prepared the prophecy. Christ fulfills it.

Why not during the Prophets? The prophets saw Messiah. They described Him bruised, crushed, lifted up, ruling, reigning, healing, and restoring. But the anointed One could not come while prophecy was still being spoken.

Prophecies must precede their fulfillment.

Christ comes when the prophetic voice ceases, so His arrival becomes the answer to every prophecy ever given. The Living Word enters after the written Word is complete.

Why not during the exile? Israel suffered under Babylon and Persia. They prayed for deliverance. Christ could have come then. But if He came during exile, His mission would seem political. He did not come to overthrow nations, but to overthrow darkness. He did not come to end captivity to kingdoms but captivity to sin. He came when Israel had returned home but was spiritually empty. When their temple stood, but their hearts were dry.

When ritual replaced relationship. Then Christ comes to rebuild not buildings, but people.

Why did Christ come during the Roman Empire? Rome provided a universal language (Greek). For the first time. The world could understand one message. The Gospel could travel through language barriers with supernatural speed. They provided an international road system. Rome's roads connected continents.

The apostles could reach Asia, Africa, Europe in one lifetime. It was a unified empire instead of dozens of tribal kingdoms, the ancient world was under one government. A single spark could ignite a global flame in a spiritually hungry world.

Rome brought order, but not meaning. Philosophy could not fill the human soul. Paganism left people empty. Mystery religions brought fear, not freedom. Israel was ready. The Gentiles were desperate. Their religious system was corrupt. Christ came when the leaders of Israel had become political, ritualistic, self-righteous, blind, oppressive, hypocritical.

He came when the temple was a market and worship was a transaction. He came when people needed not more religion, but God Himself.

Christ came after 400 years of silence. Between Malachi and Matthew, Heaven was wordless. No prophets. No angels. No fresh revelation. This silence created a hunger that no ritual could feed.

God waited until Israel stopped listening. Prophets had ceased. religion had hardened. The world was tired. hope had dimmed. Then Christ came like thunder after a long drought.

Heaven broke its silence, with a baby's cry.

The Fullness of Time: Heaven's perfect alignment. The Incarnation required the Law to be in place and prophecy complete. It required that Israel was returned, and that Rome was united and Greek was common. The roads had to have been built. Religious corruption had to be exposed, and spiritual hunger was growing. The world's systems were then failing. Only then did the Father say, "**Now.**"

Christ steps into history at the exact moment where His mission can be understood, witnessed, recorded, spread, preserved, fulfilled. No earlier. No later.

Christ came on purpose, on schedule. Christ came by divine design. Christ came at the perfect moment in world history. Christ came when humanity was ready for Redemption. Christ came when religion failed but also at the same time that the world was united enough to hear Him. Christ came in the fullness of Time, by dire necessity to save mankind, and by Divine appointment. The world was out of order, and Heaven sent the One who could reorder everything.

The incarnation is not accidental. It is perfectly timed Sovereignty.

THE WORD MADE FLESH

The Moment Eternity Entered Time

Everything in this book has been leading to this chapter. All the pre-incarnate appearances... All the Old Testament signs... All the heavenly decisions... All the divine timing... *Now it happens.*

The Son who walked Eden, wrestled Jacob, spoke from fire, stood in the furnace, appeared in Daniel's visions, and commanded Heaven's armies, steps into a womb. The Eternal becomes embryonic. The Infinite becomes an infant. The One who holds galaxies is held by a teenage girl.

Nothing in all of Scripture is more shocking. "In the beginning was the Word..." (John 1:1). John does not begin with Bethlehem. He begins with Eternity. Jesus does not start in a manger. He starts in eternal existence, co-equal with the Father. John wants you to understand that Christ is not created. Christ is not a secondary deity. Christ is not just a prophet. Christ is not an Angel; He is over the Angels, the Captain of the Host of the Army of the Lord. Christ is *God.* And then— the earthquake verse: "And the Word was made flesh..." (John 1:14).

The Creator steps into Creation. The Author enters His story. The Potter becomes clay. God puts on skin. This is not myth. This is miracle.

The Infinite claimed a body. No other religion dares say that the Divine became physical.

Greek *gods* appeared *disguised* as humans. Pagan deities manifested as *illusions.* Mythical *gods* dwelt in the sky. But Christ took on bones, blood, DNA, lungs, sweat. Hunger, fatigue, emotion, humanity and mortality. He can because He is God. He can because the Word is alive and the Word interacts with the living.

The Creator became a creature to redeem creatures back to their Creator.

Why a womb? Why 40 weeks? (nine months)? Why childhood? Christ could have arrived full-grown, with angelic fanfare, with visible glory, with thunder and fire. But He arrives through conception, through infancy, through weakness, through vulnerability, through dependence. *Why?* Christ came to redeem every stage of humanity, from conception, through pregnancy and infancy, childhood, adolescence, adulthood all the way to death. Jesus sanctifies human experience by entering into it. He redeems human life by living it.

A savior touched with the feelings of our infirmities...

Mary's womb becomes the meeting place of Heaven and Earth. The overshadowing of the Holy Spirit is the greatest miracle since Creation. What was formed inside Mary was not merely a baby. It was uncreated God, perfect humanity, divinity and flesh. It was eternity and time. It was Spirit and matter. It was Heaven and Earth. It was all that and it was all united in one Person.

Christ did not become 50% God and 50% man. He is 100% God and 100% man in one indivisible Person.

Christ had to become human because the incarnation is required for redemption of humanity. Only a man could die for mankind. Only God could bear infinite sin. Christ became man to take humanity's place. Christ remained God to bear humanity's weight. He is representation before God. Christ is the Second Adam. He is the Perfect Man. He is the true Image of God.

What Adam destroyed, Christ restores.

He became man for mediation. A mediator must touch both sides. Christ touches Heaven and Earth at the same time.

He did it for revelation. Christ shows us the Father **"He who has seen Me has seen the Father."** You want to know what God is like? Look at Jesus.

The Incarnation is not weakness, it's strategy. Satan never expected God to arrive in flesh. He never imagined the Almighty would enter the battlefield as a baby. Christ hides His Glory… not to shrink it, but to strike the enemy from an unexpected angle. He slips behind enemy lines through a womb. He grows up unnoticed. He blends in. He waits for the appointed moment. This is divine infiltration.

He that hath my commandments, and keepeth them, he it is that loveth me: and he that loveth me shall be loved of my Father, and I will love him, and will manifest myself to him. (John 14:21)

The Incarnation is war strategy.

The Word became flesh and dwells among us John says "…and dwelt among us." The Greek word *eskēnōsen* means tabernacled, pitched His tent, lived as one of us. This is Exodus language. Christ is the new tabernacle— where God lives with His people.

Everywhere Christ walks is holy ground. Bethlehem becomes holy. Nazareth becomes holy. Galilee becomes holy. Capernaum becomes holy. His presence turns ordinary places into divine encounters.

Heaven rejoices and hell trembles when Christ is born. angels erupt in praise. shepherds worship. wise men travel. prophets speak. creation responds. But also Herod rages, demons stir, hell panics, Satan understands that the One who has come is the One who will end him. This is not a sentimental nativity story. This is a cosmic confrontation.

The incarnation is the opening salvo of Heaven's invasion of Earth.

This matters because everything that follows— every miracle, parable, healing, teaching, confrontation, every cross, burial, resurrection, ascension, every future kingdom— all depends on this moment. God became human. The pre-incarnate Christ has now entered history. The eternal Son becomes Jesus of Nazareth.

He is now God among us. God with us; God as one of us. Not temporarily, but forever. Eternity past is now connected, the very moment Heaven enters Earth.

I, WISDOM, WAS THERE

The Pre-Incarnate Christ in Proverbs 8

Before mountains rose, before oceans formed, before the first beam of light pierced the darkness, Christ stood beside the Father, as Wisdom eternal, co-creating the universe.

Proverbs 8 is not poetic metaphor. It is revelation. It is Christ speaking, long before Bethlehem, long before flesh, long before Time. This is Wisdom personified. not an attribute, not an abstraction, but a divine Person.

The early Church understood it. The apostles understood it. The Hebrew sages perceived it dimly. Heaven reveals it plainly. Wisdom = Christ before the incarnation.

The LORD possessed Me in the beginning of His way before His works of old. (Proverbs 8:22)

Christ says, "The LORD possessed Me in the beginning of His way, before His works of old." This does NOT mean God "created" the Son. The Hebrew conveys that the "The LORD had Me, held Me, was united with Me." This is eternal relationship, not origin story. Before anything was made, Christ stood as God's Wisdom, God's Architect, God's Companion, God's Son, God's Delight. The Trinity is revealed not through theology books but through Scripture's earliest poetry.

When He prepared the heavens, I was there. (Proverbs 8:27)

Christ continues, "When He prepared the heavens, I was there." "I was there" means present, active and participating. Christ was architecting. He was witnessing and delighting and being a delight. This means He was doing it efficiently and correctly. He was not merely watching; He was working. John 1:3 echoes this truth:

All things were made through Him. (John 1:3)

Not some things, but all things. Every star, every galaxy, every atom, every law of physics bears the fingerprint of the Christ of God.

I was daily His delight... (Proverbs 8:30)

This is one of the most intimate statements in Scripture: "Then I was daily His delight, rejoicing always before Him."

This is Eternal Love language. Christ was not only with the Father— He was loved by the Father. His daily delight. Eternal joy. Infinite communion. Before God ever delighted in humanity, He delighted in His Son. Before God walked with Adam in the cool of the day, He walked with Christ in Eternity. Before God rested on the seventh day, Christ rested in the Father's heart.

Wisdom at Creation is Christ's creative identity. Proverbs 8 shows the Son as Co-Creator. He formed the worlds beside the Father. He is Master Builder. The Hebrew phrase *amon* means artisan, craftsman, architect. Christ is the divine engineer of everything that exists. Everything, even scientific stuff like gravity, light, DNA and the beauty of the Earth, to include the oceans and galaxies. Even life itself.

Delight of the Father. Creation is an overflow of divine joy— the joy between Father and Son. The joy of the Lord is my strength.

There is a logic behind this reality. It is the Logos = Word = Wisdom = Reason. The order of the universe flows from Him.

Proverbs 8 must be seen as Christ because the alternative interpretation collapses under its own weight. Wisdom is a Person. Those who read my books know that I always capitalize it, and this is why. "Wisdom" cannot be a mere attribute (attributes are not "brought forth"). Wisdom is not a mere poetic device. Poetry cannot create worlds. Solomon was wise but he didn't create Wisdom, although he was imbued with it. Solomon didn't predate Creation, but Wisdom did; Jesus did. The Word did. The Logos did.

Human wisdom didn't exist yet, because humans didn't yet exist. Only a divine, eternal Person fits. Only Christ matches eternity, divinity. Wisdom (even though she's called a *she* in Proverbs probably for the very reason is that *She* was creating. She took her role in Creation. She is the Father's delight. Wisdom is the Logos identity and a New Testament revelation. (FYI: And this is the truth, Wisdom is called she because the Greek and Latin words for Wisdom are feminine in gender.)

This is why the early Church universally saw Proverbs 8 as Christ. Dear Reader: You are now standing in ancient revelation.

Christ is not only Redeemer. He is Creator. Not only Savior. He is Architect. He is not only the Lamb. He is the Wisdom of God and the Power of God (1 Cor 1:24). Understanding Christ as Wisdom restores awe, deepens worship, enlarges prayer, expands identity, strengthens theology, anchors our faith in Eternity, reveals Christ's mind and intent.

How many times have you looked up something online and opened to a page or a house or a business where there is the question, Is this your business? Is this your house? Is this your webpage? Knowing that Christ is Wisdom shows us that when He approaches us especially in our need for salvation, or whatever we need from Him that what He will do for us is not just a repair job, it's the Creator reclaiming what He made. **We are His creation. We are His business. We are His house.**

The alpha reality is that Christ's eternity is not theoretical. It is practical, functional, creative, active. He was there. He was working. He was delighted in. God saw over and again, **It was good.** He was Christ even then. He is Alpha. He is Origin. He is Beginning. Before we see Him walk on water, we see Him create the waters. Before we see Him calm storms, we see Him design the laws of wind and wave. Before we see Him heal Creation, we see Him build creation. This is Christ— from everlasting to everlasting.

Before the mountains were brought forth, or ever thou hadst formed the earth and the world, even from everlasting to everlasting, thou art God. (Psalm 90:2)

WHERE THE CHRIST WENT

What He Came to Fix

When we look at the Old Testament through the lens of Christ, we discover that the Son of God did not simply appear in Bethlehem. He was already moving in the story long before the Incarnation, stepping into specific places and moments where something was broken and needed to be set right. Each appearance reveals why He came and what He came to accomplish, long before His name was spoken in a manger.

1. Eden — where fellowship was broken. In the Garden, humanity hid, ashamed and afraid, and God walked among them calling out, "Where are you?" The problem here was **disruption of relationship**. Christ came to restore the lost fellowship between God and mankind.

Even in Eden, He clothed them with skins, foreshadowing the covering that His own sacrifice would provide. The One who walked in the cool of the day came to undo the alienation caused by sin.

2. With Hagar — where the unseen woman felt abandoned. In the wilderness, Hagar believed she and her child were forgotten and were going to die there. But "the Angel of the LORD" — the pre-incarnate Christ — found her, spoke to her, and named her son. The problem was **rejection and despair**, and Christ appeared as "the God who sees." He came to restore dignity to the forgotten, to bring the outcast into God's story, and to prove that no wilderness is too remote for His compassion.

Sarah, the same woman who had put Abraham together with Hagar was the very woman who made Abraham exile her and the boy, Ishmael. God rescued them and sent them back. It was God's way of saying who your father is important. **"Hagar, you must go back — because you and your son have a place in My story, and I refuse to let you disappear."** Not punishment. Not patriarchy or hierarchy, but preservation, protection, promise, and purpose.

3. With Abraham, where covenant and future were uncertain, the Angel of the LORD appeared repeatedly to Abraham: calling him, promising him, correcting him, testing him. The issue here was **direction and assurance**. Christ came to secure the covenant Himself, to guarantee the promises of God, and to reveal that the future of salvation rests not on human strength but on divine faithfulness. He is the One who stayed Abraham's hand and provided the ram — showing that God Himself would provide the Lamb. Covenant with a man in the Earth needed to be established, or re-established. Melchizedek came to see to it Himself. Between Adam and Abraham, only Noah had a covenant — but Abraham is the first man since Eden with a personal, relational covenant binding Heaven and Earth.

4. With Jacob, where identity was twisted and character was broken, the Divine Wrestler met Jacob, at Peniel, in the dark. The problem was **a man living by deceit and fear**, striving in his own strength. Christ came there to transform Jacob into Israel, to break the old identity and give him a new one. The limp Jacob carried afterward was not defeat but redemption — the mark of one who had finally surrendered to the God who fights for him. Since the King of Salem had ratified that covenant with Abraham, this was the family. Jacob had just spent 20 years with Laban reinforcing bad bloodline traits. For all these reasons, Jacob needed to be set right.

5. With Moses, where leadership felt inadequate and bondage was crushing, The Christ of God appeared to Moses in the burning bush, in the cloud, on the mountain, and at the tent of meeting. The problem was **the oppression of God's people** and the weakness of God's chosen leader. Christ came to reveal that deliverance belongs to the Lord, not human skill. He empowered Moses, confronted Pharaoh, and led Israel out with a mighty hand, showing that redemption is not an idea but an invasion of Grace.

6. With Joshua, where conquest required divine presence standing as the Commander of the LORD's Army, Christ met Joshua outside Jericho. The issue was **a battle too great for human strategy**. Christ came to lead, not assist. His sword drawn, He revealed that victory belongs to the Lord, and that Israel's role was obedience, not self-reliance.

7. In the furnace with the three , where faith met fire. Shadrach, Meshach, and Abednego stood alone, the pre-incarnate Christ stepped into the flames. The problem here was **tyranny, idolatry, and threat of death**. Christ came to show that God is present in the suffering of His people and that He alone is worthy of worship. Personally, for those three, God came to tell and show that those who believe steadfastly on Him will be saved from evil consequences even though they may wax bold, or be very near. And He came to show His power of Salvation to onlookers who didn't even know Him.

In every one of these places, something was broken: fellowship, identity, hope, leadership, protection, or faith. And in each one, **Christ stepped in to fix what humanity could not**, pointing toward the day when He would enter the world once and for all to heal it from within. Because He goes where things are broken.

CHRIST THE CREATOR KING

Maker of Worlds, Upholder of All Things

Creation is not simply something Christ witnessed. Creation is something Christ authored. He did not arrive after the universe. The universe arrived through Him. He did not step into an already-built world and pretend that He "discovered" it, as too many men throughout history have done. The world exists because He spoke. He spoke and all the elements listened, heard, and obeyed.

The Scriptures refuse to let us miss it.

All things were made by Him; and without Him was not anything made that was made. (John 1:3)

All things were made by Him…" John does not whisper this. He declares it with thunder: Christ is not *one agent* of Creation. He is the exclusive agent. The verse is airtight. It leaves no theological wiggle room. If it exists, He created it. If it was made, He made it. If it has being, He gave it being. He is the Creator, not the created. He is the Origin, not the outcome. He is the Cause, not the consequence.

Therefore, can we now see the arrogance in the man who wants to rule what God created, outside of God? This is the attitude and the behavior that gets people kicked out of good places. Lucifer, for example --, out of Heaven. It's like the man who 'discovered' something that was already there trying to take it over and rule it as if he made it or discovered it.

In the New Testament, Paul strengthens the revelation of John with overwhelming clarity.

By Him were all things created, that are in heaven, and that are in earth, visible and invisible…" (Colossians 1:16)

Visible and invisible means the galaxies and gravity. It means atoms and angels. He rules time and space. His authority is over all thrones and dominions, powers and principalities. He is the Master of light and life. Nothing in the universe exists apart from Christ's creative will.

Apostle Paul goes further:

"…all things were created by Him, and *for* Him."

He is not only the Source. He is the Goal. Creation is not just through Christ. Creation is unto Christ. He is both its cause and its consummation.

The Son is the Architect of reality. When Proverbs 8 calls Him the *master craftsman*, it reveals the precision of His creative work. Everything in existence from the orbit of planets to the ratio of oxygen, to the delicacy of DNA – that's His work. The symmetry of flowers, the complexity of ecosystems, the constants of physics, the beauty of mathematics, the pattern of seasons to the capacity for consciousness was engineered by Christ.

Anyone who cannot see Christ or the Glory of His Creation, must surely not be trying. You'd have to pay someone to help you miss Christ--, unless you were in Jerusalem before His triumphal entry when the whole city missed His visitation.

Christ is not a distant deity. He is an intimate architect. He designed reality the way an artist designs a masterpiece and a composer writes symphonies.

He holds it all together.

By Him all things consist. (Colossians 1:17)

Consist means to *hold together*. Christ does not merely create. Christ sustains. Right now, at this very moment. Ironic, the scientist who think they discovered something that God created. Well, it has been revealed to them, Hallelujah! Electrons, for example, orbit nuclei because Christ commands it. Stars burn because Christ fuels them. atoms remain cohesive because He upholds them. gravity holds because He reinforces it. Time progresses because He wills it. existence remains because He sustains it. Creation they say was done by the sixth day, but it is not finished because Christ is sustaining it. It is an ongoing relationship between Christ and the universe.

If Christ ever stopped sustaining Creation for a millisecond, everything would collapse into nothing. Because of Him all things are fitly joined together, and He is the stabilizing force that holds all things together.

Creation reveals His Kingship. Christ is not only Creator. He is King; The one who creates is the one who rules. The one who designs is the one who determines. The one who originates is the one who governs. The Lord's sovereignty is not borrowed; it is intrinsic.

He does not take the throne. He **is** the throne. He does not inherit dominion; He **is** dominion. Creation is His kingdom, and He is its rightful King. Before Pilate ever asked, He was already King of Kings.

All of us know that no matter how low-key you may be, no matter if you shrink yourself for the sake of purpose or the sake of others, there will come a time when you must be who you are. There will come a time when you will declare who you are, or it will be declared for you. If we don't recognize and praise the Lord, the rocks will cry out. That dismisses the phrase dumb as a box of rocks. If rocks know who Christ is, and know to praise Him, then rocks are smarter than a whole lot of folks.

Later on, when we see Christ calming the sea, multiplying bread, raising the dead, healing the blind, or walking on water we will finally know and understand these are not "miracles" in the sense of breaking natural laws. He is not breaking the laws of nature. He is exercising authority over both what He made, and laws He wrote.

This is why Grace overwrites and supersedes the Law. The Lord God wrote the Law and Grace is the overwrite. It is better (for us). It is new and improved because of the Better Covenant.

Miracles are not violations of nature. Miracles are restoration to Christ's intended order. Those miracles are Christ reclaiming what He made. He created all things, therefore, He can command all things, redeem all things, judge all things, and recreate all things.

Christ is not just the center of salvation. He is the center of existence.

THE BREATH OF LIFE

The Son In The Garden

The Garden of Eden is often taught as the place where *God* walked with Adam. But Scripture points to something even deeper: It was the Son who walked there. The Christ of God was the God of Eden. Before the incarnation, before the manger, before the miracles, Christ was already moving among humanity. You can say, low-key if you mean it in the sense of Him visiting one, two or few at a time versus a stadium or amphitheater full of people.

He was not distant. He was not hidden. He was not waiting for Bethlehem to begin His involvement in human history. He was present. He was intimate. He was breathing life into Creation.

"Let *Us* make man in *Our* image…" (Genesis 1:26) is plural on purpose. This is not God speaking to Angels because Angels are not creators, and humans are not made in the image of God's Angels.

No, this is the eternal fellowship of Father, Son, and Spirit. The Father wills. The Son forms. The Spirit animates. Christ is not merely observing Creation; He is shaping it.

He is the One whose hands form Adam from the dust, not metaphorically, but literally.

The first face Adam saw was Christ. Imagine this moment. The Word who spoke galaxies into existence is now kneeling in the dust of Earth, forming humanity with His own hands. He shapes bones, muscles, tendons, brain, lungs, heart, eyes, skin, breath pathways, and blood vessels. And then Scripture gives us the most intimate act in all Creation. And He breathed into his nostrils the breath of life, (Genesis 2:7).

Whose breath?

Christ's.

The breath that enters Adam is the same breath that will later say, **"Lazarus, come forth." "Peace, be still." "Your faith has made you whole." "It is finished." "Receive the Holy Spirit.** *"*

Adam's first inhale was the breath of Christ.

Then, Genesis 3:8 says, "They heard the *voice* of the LORD God walking in the garden…" Voices do not walk; persons do. This is the first theophany in Scripture. It is a visible, embodied appearance of Christ prior to Bethlehem. Adam and Eve did not hide from a sound. They hid from *Someone*.

They hid from Someone they recognized. Someone they conversed with daily. Someone whose footsteps they knew. Someone who walked in fellowship with them. The only other Someone in this Garden, so they didn't have to ask or wonder, *Who Dat?* This Someone was Christ, the Word made present long before He was made flesh.

The Son was the one who asked the first human questions after the fall, the voice, the Person, the Christ of God. And these are the three devastating questions He asked Adam.

- **"Where are you?"**

- **"Who told you that you were naked?"**

- **"What is this you have done**?"

These are not inquiries for information. They are invitations to confession. Christ is not merely the Creator. Here, He reveals Himself as the first Shepherd, calling fallen humanity back to Himself. And He is also the first Evangelist, for in the midst of judgment He speaks the first prophecy:

The seed of the woman will crush the serpent's head.
(Genesis 3:15)

This is Christ speaking about Himself. He is the promised Seed. He is the serpent-crusher. He is the redeemer already preparing salvation. He knows this because He is not limited by Time or space and because He knows All Things.

Even in Eden, Christ is both Judge and Savior.

The Son was the one who clothed them. Genesis 3:21 says ,"The LORD God made coats of skins, and clothed them." This is the first sacrifice in human history. Blood spilled. An innocent life was given. A covering was provided. It is the pre-incarnate Christ, the eternal Lamb, who performs it.

Christ Himself slays the animal, prepares the skin, covers their shame, and foreshadows the Cross. Adam and Eve wore a prophetic symbol of the Lamb who would one day cover sin permanently.

From the first sin, Christ becomes the One who atones.

Eden reveals Christ's heart for humanity. In Eden we see His creativity, His ingenuity, His intimacy, His authority, His compassion, His justice, and His Mercy. He foreshadows the Promise and reveals Himself again as Provider – even seeing that the needs of His Creation has just changed.

He pursued after Adam and Eve; Christ did not start loving humanity in the Gospels. He loved humanity at Creation. He didn't suddenly become the Lord, My

Shepherd from David's mouth in the Psalms, or the Good Shepherd in John 10; He was the Shepherd of Eden.

He didn't suddenly become the Lamb of God at the Jordan River. He was the Lamb in Genesis 3. He didn't suddenly become the Word made flesh. He was the Word walking in the Garden. Christ showed us His Love and who He is; His real identity long before Jesus of Nazareth appears on the pages of history.

The Christ of Eden is the Christ of the Gospels. He is the Christ of Revelation. He is the Christ of God.

MELCHIZEDEK

Priest Of The Most High God

The First Priest-King, and a Revelation of Christ Before Bethlehem is the King of Salem, Melchizedek. He appears suddenly, without introduction. Without genealogy. Without origin story. Without conclusion. Melchizedek steps into Scripture like a lightning flash carrying bread, carrying wine, carrying blessing, carrying mystery.

Genesis 14 gives us only a handful of verses, but they thunder across the whole Bible. Everything about Melchizedek refuses to fit the category of a normal human king.

He stands alone in Scripture a priest before there was a priesthood, a king before Israel had a king, a worshiper of God before Abraham's covenant was even formed. Melchizedek is not merely a historical figure. He is a revelation. A foreshadowing. A manifestation. A Christological pattern so powerful that even the Book of Hebrews breathes awe when mentioning him.

King of Righteousness and King of Peace. His very name is a sermon Melchi = King. Tzedek = righteousness. Melchizedek means: King of Righteousness. But he is also called, King of Salem.

Salem = Shalom = Peace. So, he is King of Righteousness. King of Peace. These are not titles given lightly. Nowhere else in Scripture is any man called King of Righteousness. Except one: Christ Himself.

Isaiah prophesies Him as "Prince of Peace." Melchizedek mirrors Christ's dual identity as the One who brings righteousness to humanity and peace to the universe. This is no accident. This is revelation.

He is Priest of the Most High God. Before Levi ever existed, Melchizedek is the first priest in the Bible. The Levitical priesthood comes 400 years later.

That means Melchizedek's priesthood is older, higher, purer, and not based on genealogy. Hebrews 7 emphasizes this repeatedly: "Without father, without mother, without descent…" —not because he literally had none, but because Scripture intentionally omits it to make him a type of the Eternal Son.

The Levitical priests were priests by birth. Melchizedek was priest by divine appointment. And so is Christ.

He brings bread and wine long before Passover. Long before Jesus lifts the cup in the Upper Room. Long before the Cross.

Melchizedek brings out bread, wine, and the blessing. This is the first communion in the Bible. And who does he serve it to? Not Israel. Israel doesn't exist yet. He didn't serve it to a priest; no priesthood exists yet. Not a king; Abraham isn't royalty. He serves it to Abram, the Father of Faith.

The message is clear: Before the covenant, before the Law, before the priesthood, Christ foreshadows the Cross through Melchizedek's hands. Bread for Christ's body. Wine for Christ's Blood. Abraham eats the first prophetic communion with the pre-incarnate pattern of Christ standing before him.

He blesses Abram, not the other way around. Genesis 14 says, "He blessed him and said..." *"Blessed be Abram of the Most High God..."*

Here is the pattern: The greater blesses the lesser. And Hebrews 7 confirms: "Without contradiction the less is blessed of the better." This means Melchizedek is greater than Abraham. And if he is greater than Abraham, he is greater than Levi, greater than Aaron, greater than Moses. His priesthood stands above all.

Which is why Hebrews says: "Thou art a priest forever after the order of Melchizedek." Christ is not a Levitical priest. He is a Melchizedekian priest, eternal, heavenly, royal, without beginning or ending.

Abram tithes to Him. Abram gives Melchizedek a tenth of all he has. This is the first tithe in the Bible, and he doesn't give it to a man, but to a divine representative.

Why?

Because Abram recognizes he is standing before Someone greater than himself. Someone divine. Someone priestly. Someone kingly. If Melchizedek were merely a local king, Abraham would never tithe to him. This act reveals Abraham's profound understanding that he is honoring Christ's eternal priesthood through Melchizedek.

Was Melchizedek Christ Himself?

Theologians fall into two camps:

The firsts group says that Melchizedek was a Christophany, a pre-incarnate appearance of Christ Himself. This view sees no genealogy, eternal priesthood, King of Righteousness, King of Peace, receiving tithes, blessing Abraham, bringing bread and wine. All as direct evidence of Christ appearing in human form.

The second camp says Melchizedek was a human king used as a type of Christ. This view says Scripture intentionally removes His ancestry. To make Him a prophetic shadow of Christ, not Christ literally. But here is the revelation, whichever view you take, Melchizedek reveals Christ, His role, His offices, His identity, His authority.

He is either Christ appearing before Bethlehem, OR the clearest prophetic window into the Christ to come. Either way, Melchizedek stands unmatched in Scripture as the priest-king pattern of Jesus. Christ MUST be seen in Melchizedek. Because this is where we learn Christ is Priest before the Cross, King before the manger, Blessing Giver before Abraham, Communion Host before Calvary, Eternal Priest before Levi, Royal Authority before David, Divine Representative before Israel. Melchizedek is not a side-story. He is a revelation. He shows that Christ's priesthood is not temporary, not human, not inherited, not limited, not earthly, but eternal, Heavenly, Sovereign.

This is the Christ of God long before He walked among us.

` Abram met Melchizedek before he ever became Abraham. Before circumcision, before Isaac, before the covenant was cut, the Priest-King of Heaven met a man still becoming who God said he would be. Christ, in the order of Melchizedek, blesses us not after we are perfected, but while we are still Abram. While we are still in process, unfinished, while we are still *becoming*, on the way to Abraham.

CAPTAIN OF THE LORD'S ARMY

Joshua's Encounter with Pre-Incarnate Christ

The conquest of Canaan was not merely a military campaign, it was a divine reclamation. It was a spiritual war, a kingdom collision. And before Joshua ever lifted a sword, Christ Himself appeared not as a lamb, not as a teacher, not as a gentle comforter, but as a warrior. This is one of the clearest pre-incarnate appearances of Christ in the entire Old Testament and one of the most misunderstood.

Joshua 5:13 tells us that a Man stood opposite him with His sword drawn in His hand." Not sheathed. Not resting. Not symbolic. A man with His sword drawn, ready for battle is the Captain of the Lord's Army.

Joshua is no coward, but even he approaches cautiously, "Are You for us, or for our adversaries?" And the answer is a revelation **"No; but as Captain of the Host of the LORD. I Am now come."**

In other words, *I'm not here to take your side. I'm here for My side.* Christ is not the mascot of human causes. He is the Commander of Heaven's armies. Joshua Falls to the Ground and Worships. Joshua responds in a way that would get any Israelite executed if the figure were an angel.

"Joshua fell on his face to the earth and worshiped."

Angels reject worship. All of them. Every time. Without exception. But this Being receives Joshua's worship. This can only be God, the LORD, the pre-incarnate Christ. No angel, prophet, or created being ever accepts worship in Scripture.

Only Christ. **"Take off your shoes…"** — The proof that this is Christ

The Being speaks, **"Take off your shoes from your feet, for the place where you stand is holy."** This is identical to God's command to Moses at the burning bush. Identical phrasing. Identical revelation. Identical presence. Where Christ stands, the ground becomes holy.

This is the same Christ who later says, **"Where two or three are gathered in My name, there am I."**

Presence makes a place holy, not geography. Joshua is standing in a battlefield, but because Christ is there, it becomes a sanctuary.

Christ appears as a warrior because Joshua's real battle is not with Jericho, it is with the unseen realm. The Captain appears because angels are about to fight walls are about to fall, territory is about to shift. Demonic strongholds are about to crumble. The land is about to be consecrated back to God. The conquest of Canaan was spiritual long before it was physical. Christ stands before Joshua to say, **"I fight the battles you cannot see."** This is consistent with the Old Testament revelation, **"The Lord is a man of war; the Lord is His name."** (Exodus 15:3)

"Christ triumphed over principalities and powers."
(Colossians 2:15)

"And heaven opened, and behold a white horse…"
(Revelation 19:11)

The Warrior Christ appears in Joshua before He appears in Revelation. Christ's Sword in His hand is symbolic of judgment, authority, truth, spiritual war, and divine dominion. This is the same Christ who later says, **"I did not come to bring peace, but a sword."**

He didn't come to bring violence, but division between Truth and deception. This is the same Christ in Revelation whose sword comes from His mouth--, His Word. Sharp. Piercing. Able to divide cleanly, quickly.

Christ commands the battle plan. Joshua does not strategize; Christ does. Christ orchestrates seven priests, seven trumpets, seven days, seven circuits ,a divine shout, and finally, a supernatural collapse.

Why?

Because Jericho's fall is not military genius or prowess. It is divine demonstration. If we think about the battles in life that we try to win by complicated, expensive, and time-consuming man-made solutions that can't even be overcome that way, Wisdom would make us pause. Just a simple solution from the Lord would have crushed that entire problem in a few days, because it was spiritual. When a problem is spiritual nothing in the natural can solve it. Adam and Eve's nakedness in the Garden was spiritual. Those natural leaves couldn't hide it or their shame. But the animal blood sacrifice was the spiritual solution. So, who knew?

The Christ of God knew. That's who knew.

Christ orchestrates the battle to show that victory comes from God, not human strength. He is not just the God who commands worship. He is the God who commands war.

This chapter has revealed another dimension of Christ that modern believers could ignore. Christ is a warrior. Christ is a commander. Christ is a strategist. Christ confronts. Christ fights. Christ wins.

The Lord, My Shepherd is not only the Shepherd or the Teacher, or the Healer, although He is all that. But He is also the Captain of Hosts, the Crusher of Serpents, the Lord of Heaven's Armies, the Rider on the White Horse, the Lion of Judah, the King Who Wages War In Righteousness. Even pre-incarnate, long before Jesus walked the Earth, He stood in armor. He is not just the Lamb of God. He is the Captain of the LORD's Armies.

This is Christ. the fierce, commanding, strategic Christ of God. He is the same Christ who overturns tables, casts out demons, rebukes storms, and conquers Hell itself. This is the Christ who leads Joshua into battle. This is the Christ who leads His Church now.

THE FOURTH MAN IN THE FIRE

Christ in the Furnace with Shadrach, Meshach, and Abednego

The Babylonian furnace is one of the most dramatic scenes in the entire Old Testament. Three young faithful, fearless, and unbending Hebrew men stand before the most powerful king on Earth and refuse to bow. The real revelation begins not in their courage, not in the king's rage, not in the heat of the flames... ...but in the presence of a **fourth** Man. This is not a symbolic vision. This is not an angelic rescue squad; this is a Christophany. This is the pre-incarnate Christ walking in the fire with His faithful.

Lo, I see four men loose, walking in the fire,
and the form of the fourth is like the Son of God.
(Daniel 3:25)

Nebuchadnezzar didn't know His name, but he knew His nature.

They were thrown into Fire. *Why a fire?* Fire was Babylon's evil answer because they refused to bow to Nebuchadnezzar's image. (Daniel 3).

Nebuchadnezzar demanded worship. This worship would have been an initiation; so be careful what you bow to you in your real life. Nebuchadnezzar wanted what God gets; their worship. The evil Babylonish king wanted their souls. He wanted their allegiance. And when he couldn't get it, he tried to incinerate them.

The three Hebrews refused, and he escalated the punishment to fire, which was one of the most feared executions in the ancient world.

Babylon's main deities were Marduk (Bel), Nabu, Ishtar, Nergal (God of the underworld) and Tammuz. Child sacrifice was not a routine part of Babylonian worship, that was more Canaanite/Moabite/Phoenician, so we cannot surmise the Nebuchadnezzar was using these young men for child sacrifice. Historically he was *not* performing a Molech/Chemosh ritual.

But Babylon was the prototype of all anti-God systems (Revelation 17–18). In Babylon, fire, furnaces, and burning WERE used for punishment, of course, but also in rituals related to purification, initiation, judgment, and for the appeasement of the idol *gods* they served.

The three Hebrews were being punished for loyalty to Yahweh, forced to undergo a trial by fire, confronted by demonic authority structures, publicly shamed, spiritually challenged, and being used as a spectacle to intimidate others for behavior modification.

It *was* a **demonic power-play**.

This is a big problem, and this is why Jesus showed up in the fire. This was a spiritual problem, it is a faceoff of spiritual kingdoms. these three young men were in covenant with Heaven, with Yahweh, So, Heaven responded by sending The Son of God (Daniel 3:25), a pre-incarnate Christophany. This would be a Heavenly interruption to a demonic ritual.

Even though they were in exile, the three Hebrew boys were still faithful and constant. So whatever you're going through in life, look at their pattern. They were under a godless king. There was a demonic image that they were commanded to worship. This was a false worship system, so they wouldn't acquiesce. The furnace was a fiery altar that demanded sacrifice. Maybe there is no fire in the natural, but you may feel like you are really going through, then call on the Son of God to be with you as you go through and there will have to be a spiritual showdown and then a miraculous deliverance.

Shadrach, Meshach, and Abednego in the fire is another appearance of the pre-incarnate Christ, a preview that the One who walks with us in earthly flames is the same One who keeps us from the eternal fire. The Fourth

Man in the fire was Christ showing, ahead of time, that He alone can keep a soul from burning in Hell.

Sometimes obedience throws you into heat, pressure, danger, accusation, or flames. In addition to the Fourth Man showing up, Yahweh didn't allow Shadrach, Meshach, and Abednego to be punished; instead, they too were being revealed. They stepped into the fire because the fire was where Christ intended to show Himself. Faith does not mean avoiding flames. Faith means finding Christ wherever you have to step.

Christ appears when the fire is hottest. The furnace was heated seven times hotter and that was human wrath at its peak. Everything about this scene screams death. The furnace roars, even the soldiers die from the heat, then the flames engulfed the faithful, but Christ arrives.

He does not always meet His people *before* the fire. He often meets them *in* the fire. Because the flames burn away everything that hides His presence. No one saw the Fourth Man until they were inside. Nebuchadnezzar saw a Divine Companion. The king testifies. "I see four men… and the fourth looks like the Son of God." This is not poetry. This is a literal vision. Nebuchadnezzar recognized divine presence, supernatural calm, unearthly glory, protective power, and companionship in crisis. The fire did not reveal their destruction. It revealed their Deliverer.

The flames became a stage for Christ's appearance. Christ loosens what the fire tries to bind. "They fell down bound... but were walking loose."

The only thing the fire destroyed was the ropes that held them. This is Christ's fire-math:

- Heat removes bondage but never harms identity.
- Fire burns ropes, not people.
- What the enemy meant to kill you becomes the place Christ sets you free.

Christ did not keep them out of the furnace. He kept them from being consumed by it.

Christ walks. He was not hovering, He was on the ground walking right with those Hebrew boys. He was not hovering. He was not spectating Daniel notes that they were walking in the fire. Walking means calm, deliberate, unhurried, unhurt, unharmed, and fearless. Christ is not frantic in crisis. He is majestic. He walks where others burn. He strides where others fear.

He stands where others fall. Christ is not merely present in your fire; He is comfortable in it. Hint: He made it; He can command it. It must obey Him.

Not even the smell of smoke when the three came out. Not a hair singed, not a garment harmed, not even the smell of smoke on them. This is the miracle behind the miracle. Christ's presence does not just preserve you, it preserves your identity, your dignity, your future.

When He brings you out, no one will be able to tell you were ever in a fire. Your testimony will not be damage— your testimony will be deliverance.

Christ reveals himself only to the faithful. Christ was not visible to the soldiers. Not visible to the crowd. Not visible to Babylon. Only those who had faith to stand, faith to refuse the idol, faith to endure the furnace, faith to obey God— only they saw Him up close. Babylon watched from outside, but the faithful saw Him inside.

Some people only see Christ's works. The faithful see Christ Himself.

Christ in the furnace reveals His solidarity with the suffering. His power over impossible situations. His presence in persecution. His identity as Deliverer. His fire-proof protection. His companionship in crisis. His willingness to appear when all seems lost. His delight in standing with the faithful because He is faithful. He is not a fake friend. His supremacy over kings and kingdoms. This is the same Christ who later says, "**I am with you always.**" He meant it literally, and Shadrach, Meshach, and Abednego experienced it literally.

The Christ of the Gospels is the Christ of the furnace. The Christ who hung on a cross is the Christ who walks in fire. The Christ who saves is the Christ who stands with His people in every flame of life.

Before He ever came in the flesh, Christ stepped into Babylon's furnace to make a statement: **'If I can**

keep you in this fire, I can keep you from the fire to come."

And of some have compassion, making a difference: And others save with fear, pulling them out of the fire; hating even the garment spotted by the flesh. (Jude 1:22-23)

THE ANCIENT OF DAYS

Daniel's Vision of the Son of Man

Daniel saw what few humans have ever seen, the Heavenly Courtroom: the Throne of the Eternal God, and the radiant figure who approached Him with authority, glory, and power. In this chapter we enter one of the most breathtaking, Christ-centered visions in all Scripture. Daniel 7 is not symbolic myth. It is not prophetic poetry, it is a literal glimpse into the Eternal Throne Room.

Before Christ ever took on flesh. "The Ancient of Days" — The Eternal Father on the Throne. Daniel describes the Father as sitting on a fiery throne, clothed in snow-white garments, hair white like pure wool, radiating glory, attended by millions of Angels, presiding in judgment.

This is God the Father— Eternal, pure, Holy, unchanging. But the vision does not end there. The Ancient of Days is on the throne… and Someone approaches Him. Someone with divine authority. Someone with eternal Glory. Someone worshiped by nations. Who could possibly walk toward the Ancient of Days and receive dominion?

Only One. "One Like the Son of Man" — The Pre-Incarnate Christ Daniel writes:

> "I saw… One like the Son of Man coming with the clouds of heaven." (Daniel 7:13)

Notice the language "One like…" = a visible, human-like form "Son of Man" = Christ's favorite title for Himself, "with the clouds" = a divine signature (only God rides on clouds; see Psalm 104:3). This is Christ before Bethlehem. He is appearing in the Glory that He shared with the Father "before the world was" (John 17:5). The Son approaches the Father… and Heaven watches.

Christ receives the Kingdom, not an Earthly kingdom, but the Eternal one. Daniel continues "And there was given Him dominion, and glory, and a kingdom…" Given by whom?

By the Ancient of Days.

Christ does not seize the Kingdom. He receives it from the Father as His eternal inheritance. This confirms The Son is distinct from the Father. The Son is equal in glory. The Son is eternal in nature. The Son is the rightful ruler of all nations. The Father enthrones the Son, publicly, eternally, universally. This is the real coronation, the heavenly reality behind all earthly authority.

All nations worship Him. Daniel 7:14 reveals something staggering. "...all peoples, nations, and languages should serve Him." "Serve" here is the Aramaic word *pelach*, which is a term used only of divine worship in the Old Testament. Daniel is not describing political obedience. He is describing worship.

Only God is worshiped. So, if the Son is worshiped, the Son is God. This is one of the clearest proofs in Scripture of the deity of Christ before His Bethlehem incarnation.

His Dominion Is Everlasting Daniel says the Lord's dominion is everlasting. It shall not pass away. His Kingdom shall never be destroyed. This is not Israel's temporary monarchy. This is not Rome's empire. This is not a prophetic season. This is the eternal reign of Christ. The Lamb slain before the foundation of the world is also the King enthroned before the foundation of the world.

Daniel saw Christ's deity long before the New Testament, The Jews of Jesus' day understood Daniel 7. They knew exactly what "Son of Man" meant. It meant deity, authority, kingship, divinity, heavenly glory, and eternal rule.

So, when Jesus called Himself "the Son of Man," He wasn't claiming humanity. He was claiming Daniel 7 divinity. This is why the high priest tore his robe when Jesus said **"You will see the Son of Man coming with the clouds of heaven**. (John 14:62)

He was quoting Daniel 7, declaring Himself the One Daniel saw. This was not speaking of the future; it was not symbolic or metaphor; it was literal.

The chiastic echo: The Son approaches the Throne in Daniel, and returns on clouds in Revelation. Daniel sees the Son of Man approaching the Father. Revelation sees the Son of Man returning to Earth. The pattern is perfect:

- Daniel 7 — the Son approaches Heaven's throne.
- Revelation 1 — the Son appears in blazing glory.
- Revelation 14 — the Son comes on the clouds.
- Revelation 19 — the Son returns as Warrior-King

Christ's story is not linear. It is eternal. It arcs from eternity past to eternity future.

Daniel 7 is the cornerstone for understanding Christ's eternal identity, His divine nature, Christ's Heavenly authority, Kingship, and Messiahship. Christ's relationship with the Father. Christ's destiny over nations, and His unending rule. This is Christ before the Cross, before humility, before flesh. This is Christ in Glory. If we only know the Christ of the Gospels, we know Him partially.

Daniel shows us the Christ of Eternity, the blazing King who rules the universe.

Jesus didn't *become* Christ. He **is** eternally Christ.

CLARIFICATION OF COUNCILS

Editorial Note

While not the scope of this book I did want to mention something briefly. The mention of the Divine Council of God is just that. The mention of councils deserves a little bit of discussion. A council can refer to a group of high-ranking demonic powers or a governing body of evil spirits. Of course, this has nothing to do with Jesus and the Divine Council that made the plans for Jesus to come to Earth at any kind, in any way, and especially incarnate.

The dark kingdom counterfeits the things of God. There is a council or coven in witchcraft. There is a counterfeit apostolic council. Evil councils is cultural language, testimony language, or occult hierarchy language, not biblical language since these actual words are not in the Bible.

In the Bible we do know that there is spiritual hierarchy in the kingdom of darkness. There are principalities, ruling *spirits* governing regions, powers. There are enforcers of wickedness, rulers of darkness, Territorial dominions, spiritual wickedness in high places, and high-ranking spirits influencing culture and nations. (Ephesians 6:12)

Jesus, Himself also acknowledges levels of demonic strength ("this kind..." Mark 9:29). So, hierarchy is real.

People in the occult use the number thirteen and it has become a number termed as "unlucky." In occultism, 13 symbolizes rebellion, inversion of divine order, perversion of covenant, distortion of the Last Supper. It is a mockery of the 12 tribes + Christ. Thirteen can be recognized as a counterfeit leadership structure. Occult groups choose 13 because they know God uses 12... and wouldn't they try to "one up" Him. From the dark kingdom whatever they choose is a dark imitation, not divine reality.

There are spiritual thrones, dominions, principalities, and authorities in the unseen world. They often counterfeit the kingdom of God. So, some cultures, occult systems, and deliverance ministries use terms such as "Council of 7 ". "Council of Elders". "Grand Masters" "Princes" "Powers of the Air" and other terms. None of these labels override Scripture.

Regardless of what people call it spiritual wickedness exists.

Jesus dealt with demons. Paul dealt with demons. Believers still do; they do exist. But they are *not* sovereign.

Satan is not God's opposite. He is a created being. His hierarchy is limited. Their power is permitted only for a time. They are *not* allowed to touch those under Christ's covering. In Christ we are far more powerful than they are. They are terrified of people who are walking upright in Christ in the calling of God. (Luke 10:19 1 John 5:18 Colossians 2:15 Matthew 28:18).

People with occult backgrounds often describe councils of the dark kingdom because they have either experienced it or know someone who has. They may mention terms such as:

- Council of 5

- Council of 7

- Council of 9

- Council of 12

- Council of 13

- 70 spiritual elders

- the high table

- the round table

- the grand masters

The reason the numbers vary is because they come from different cultures such as: Dominican, Haitian, African, Central American, Brazilian, and European. Occult structures all use different symbolic numbers.

Occult groups *mimic* God's structures. They twist the Trinity, the 5-fold ministry, the 7 spirits of God, the 12 tribes, the 12 apostles, the 24 elders, the 70 disciples, or the heavenly or Divine Council. So ,"5," "7," "12," and "13" show up because they are counterfeit spiritual math.

Dark kingdoms in the spiritual world operate regionally, not globally. They imitate hierarchy, but they do not unify. Not only that, they are not Omnipresent, as God is. They are not Omniscient, but God is, and they are not Omnipotent – but God is. God is all that.

So, one person's "Council of 5" and another's "Council of 13" is often based on information they've gotten from deliverance grounds or where they, themselves have a real history of witchcraft exposure. It is, however, deliverance language. It is occult survivor language. There is knowledge of the dark kingdom common among ex-witch doctors, ex-santera, ex-palo mayombe, ex-voodoo, ex-brujo/bruja practitioners, ex-cultists, and ex-New Agers. Their experience is real.

Their experiences are definitive as to why Jesus had to come to Earth for the multitudes. To save the people and set them free.

The hierarchy of the dark kingdom is from highest to lowest:

Satan is a fallen cherub, not God's equal. He is limited, not omnipresent.

Principalities (*archons*) - High-ranking territorial *spirits* over nations.

Powers (*exousia*) - Spiritual beings enforcing demonic agendas.

Rulers Of Darkness (*kosmokrators*) - Cultural and societal influencers.

Spiritual Wickedness In High Places - Occult, religious, and atmospheric *spirits*.

Demons (lesser *spirits*) - Ground-level tormentors; foot soldiers.

The kingdom of darkness is organized, so it could stand to reason that there would be groupings and structures to enact their evil in the Earth against the sons of men. Although not all knowing, all-powerful and not able to be everywhere at once, they are organized, therefore Jesus had to come to destroy the works of the dark kingdom.

Dark Kingdoms Mimic God's Kingdom. The dark kingdom produces:

False councils – copying God's Divine Council

False elders – copying the 24 elders

False apostles – copying the 12

False prophetic seers (diviners)– copying God's prophets

False healing rituals – copying God's healing

False washing rituals – copying baptism

False sacrifice systems – copying covenant

False spiritual ranks – copying God's Heavenly order

They are counterfeit. They have no original power. All they can do is imitate and distort.

Much of what those who teach on deep and serial abuse deliverance comes from talking, screaming, yelling, manifesting *spirits* during deliverance sessions. Some can come from survivors of occult systems describing what they experienced. People from African, Caribbean, or Latin American witchcraft structures. Ritual abuse testimonies, and the spiritual "maps" of trauma victims.

Deliverance-derived information is always a mix of real spiritual truths, personal experiences, cultural traditions, trauma imagery, with some demonic deception mixed in. Demons tell partial truths — often exaggerated, dramatized, symbolic, or distorted — because deception is their nature.

Ex-witches often speak of numbers like 5, 7, OR 13. Five = grace (so they counterfeit it). Seven = spiritual completion (so they distort it). Twelve = government (so they mimic it). Thirteen = rebellion (so they empower it). A "Council of 5" in one region may be a "Council of 7" in another. These are territorial "councils" That's why the numbers vary.

Those who have been exposed to thee systems often have strange dreams of councils, meetings, rituals, knowledge of things that happen in spiritual realms such as offerings, animals. They may talk of spiritual ranks. They may be under heavy spiritual oppression. They can't interpret or rightly divide Scripture, and they may experience other issues.

What some call "Councils in specific territories" coveys the way of categorizing the biblical reality of Principalities, which are regional. And the other "councils" which are territorial.

Still all those reasons, all that structure is reason for Jesus to come to Earth for mankind, to claim back what and who is His. Amen.

PRAYER OF PROTECTION

Father, in the Name of Jesus,
I stand under the covering of Christ's authority.
No counterfeit hierarchy,
no dark council,
no principality or power
has any rights to me, my life, my work, or my calling.

I reject every imitation structure
that tries to exalt itself against the knowledge of God.
Every dark authority is disarmed,
every counterfeit throne is dismantled,
every false council is silenced,
every voice that is not from You is cancelled.

I am hidden in Christ,
covered by His blood,
and sealed by the Holy Spirit.

No weapon formed against me will prosper.
In the Name of Jesus, Amen.

PRAYER OF SEVERANCE FROM OCCULT CONNECTIONS

(This is for your own cleansing if you've ever listened to ex-witch testimonies.)

Lord Jesus,
I cut myself free
from every occult structure,
every counterfeit authority,
every false council,
every spiritual hierarchy
that did not come from You.

I break all influence,
all residue,
all fear,
all fascination,
and all spiritual interference.

My spirit belongs to Christ alone.
I will not hear the voice of strangers.
I am sealed, protected, and sanctified.
In the Name of Jesus, Amen.

THE DIVINE WARRIOR

Fear Not

Do not fear is often said in the Bible. The Christ of God is fearless, He is wise, He is Omnipotent, Omniscient, Omnipresent. But mostly we should all be aware that there are names and indicators, even in the Old Testament as to who God is. As long as we are on the Lord's side, the attributes of God will work for us. I especially want to say, *The Lord is My Shepherd*. I've never known of another sheep shepherding the flock. We are the sheep of His pasture, He is not a co-sheep, although He is described as meek and mild.

God's role as Divine Warrior is one of the major Old Testament themes.

"WARRIOR" TITLES OF GOD

These are direct names or descriptions of God as a fighter, commander, or warrior.

1. **Yahweh Sabaoth (YHWH of Hosts / LORD of Hosts). Mentioned o***ver 240 times* in the Old Testament. Commander of Heaven's Armies. Conveys strategy, military power, angelic armies, and cosmic warfare.

2. **Ish Milchamah (Man of War / Warrior).** Exodus 15:3 — "The LORD is a man of war.". Direct declaration of God's identity as a warrior.

3. **Gibbor (Mighty Warrior / Champion).** Seen in Isaiah 42:13; Zephaniah 3:17. Conveys heroic strength, victory, champion-like power.

God reveals Himself to us in many ways. One of those ways is by His Names, some of which emphasize battle, judgment, or war-like action.

4. **El Shaddai — "God of Power" / "God Almighty"** Not strictly military, but used often in contexts involving, conquest, judgment, and overwhelming force. It's a "might that overthrows."

5. **El Elyon — "God Most High."** This name is used in contexts where God subdues nations (e.g., Psalm 47).

6. **El Qanna — "Jealous God."** This name is seen in covenant-war contexts; God fights spiritually for His people.

7. **YHWH Nissi — "The LORD My Banner."** Exodus 17:15–16 (after battle with Amalek). A banner is a battle standard. Means: God is the rallying point in war.

8. **YHWH Makkēh — "The LORD Who Strikes"** (Ezekiel 7:9) Refers to God as the one who executes judgment blows.

9. **YHWH Shophēt — "The LORD Who Judges"** - Judgment in ancient context is often war imagery.

The following are descriptions of God as a military leader. These are not "names" but strong descriptions used repeatedly throughout the Old Testament.

10. **"The LORD** marches like a warrior." Isaiah 42:13

11. **"The LORD** will go before you". Processional-war language (Isa 52:12).

12. **"The LORD** roars from Zion". (Amos 1:2) War-cry imagery.

13. **"The LORD** treads the winepress" (Isaiah 63:1–6) A vivid battle depiction.

14. **"The LORD** rides on the clouds" (Psalm 68:4) This was an ancient Near Eastern war-god motif repurposed to Yahweh alone.

GOD AS JUDGE-WARRIOR IN PROPHETIC LITERATURE

15. **"The LORD of Vengeance"** (El Neqamoth) (Psalm 94:1). Vengeance is judicial-war language.

16. **"The One who breaks nations"** (Jeremiah 51:20–24) God pictured as wielding His people as battle instruments.

17. **"The LORD, the Mighty One" / El Gibbor** (Isaiah 10:21) Connects to divine battle power.

GOD'S STRATEGIC OR DISRUPTIVE REPRESENTATIONS

These names and characteristic descriptions highlight that God outwits nations, overthrows kings, uses confusion, disruption, or strategy in battle. Shame, some kings don't realize that it was God that allowed them to be in power in the first place. But too many throughout history get drunk on power an the Lord ends up taking them down. The Earth is the Lord's and the fullness thereof. The Earth is still the Lord's.

18. **The LORD of the Earth** (Adon Kol Ha'aretz) - Used when God dispossesses nations.

19. **The LORD who Confounds** - Not a formal name, but God causes confusion in battle (Ex 14:24), ambush strategy (Josh 8), and fear to fall on armies (Ex 15:16; Josh 2:9).

20. **The Rock (Tzur)**, (Deut 32) Strength, fortress, defense, immovable power. A military metaphor.

21. **A Consuming Fire** (Deut 4:24; 9:3). Used in the context of destroying enemy nations.

These are 20+ distinct names, titles, or portrayals of God related to war, battle, strategy, judgment, or disruptive power.

God fights for His people. From the earliest texts, Yahweh is portrayed as a warrior who intervenes in human history.

> The LORD is a man of war; the Lord is His name.
> (Exodus 15:3)

GOD'S TITLES AS THE DIVINE WARRIOR

The Old Testament uses many names and titles that present God in military terms. These names reveal power, strategy, judgment, and protection.

- **Yahweh Sabaoth** — *Lord of Hosts* (commander of heavenly armies)

- **Ish Milchamah** — *Man of War*

- **El Gibbor** — *Mighty Warrior / Champion*

- **YHWH Nissi** — *The LORD My Banner* (battle standard)

- **A Consuming Fire** — divine conquest language

- **The Rock** — fortress and defender

God's warrior activity follows a pattern. Nearly every battle scene where God intervenes fits into a consistent 4-part pattern:

The Enemy Threatens - Whether Pharaoh, Amalek, Canaanite kings, Midian, Assyria, or Babylon, an enemy rises against God's people or God's purposes.

God Arises as Warrior. He confounds enemies, sends fear into armies, fights with heavenly hosts, gives strategy, goes before His people, and judges wicked nations.

God Wins the Victory - He delivers His people with miracles, confusion in the enemy camp, angelic intervention, direct judgments, and empowering His chosen leaders.

God is Praised as King and Warrior - Example: Miriam's song in Exodus 15, Psalms 18, 24, 68, 144, etc.

Human leaders are seen as "Warrior Extensions" of God. The OT repeatedly shows that God fights, but He fights through His **chosen** instruments. We see Moses (Exodus). Joshua's conquest. Of note are Judges like Gideon, Deborah, Samson. Certainly, David was God's warrior-king. Elijah and Elisha engaged in and were mighty in prophetic warfare.

These leaders are not independent generals; they are commissioned warriors carrying out Yahweh's strategy. God's warfare is both physical and spiritual. Pay attention to the previous sentence. This is one of the driving forces of this series: Jesus looks like He's doing something in the natural, and for all intents and purposes He is, but The Christ of God is acting spiritually in everything He does. If we can see that, we can see the Glory of God.

The Old Testament divine warfare operates on two intertwined levels. There is physical war. God defeats nations, armies, kings, empires. There is either as a precursor or simultaneously a spiritual war that bought the natural problem or supports the raging of the physical problems. Man sees the physical, the natural, feels the pain or the discomfort. Heaven sees the source of the issue and defeats it spiritually. This is why a Christ anointing is needed. It is superior to all other powers that have absconded to the dark kingdom and continue to rage war against mankind.

Behind nations are idols, false *gods*, demonic powers, and cosmic opposition known as spiritual wickedness in high places. When God defeats Egypt, Canaan, Assyria, or Babylon, He is also judging their spiritual rulers (Exodus 12:12).

Thus, divine warfare is cosmic, not merely regional.

God as Warrior is also God as Judge. His battles are always morally charged. He fights for us. He protects children, the innocent, the oppressed. He fights against injustice and idolatry. He fights to uphold His covenant.

Divine war is never capricious; it is judgment and salvation happening simultaneously.

God's warrior role is central to the Covenant. In the covenant blessings and curses (Deut. 28), if Israel obeys, God fights *for* them. If Israel rebels, God fights *against* them. This theme appears throughout Judges, Kings, and the Prophets.

The Psalms celebrate God as Warrior-King. Some of the most beautiful expressions of the motif appear here:

- "Who is this King of Glory? The LORD strong and mighty in battle." (Ps. 24:8)

- "He trains my hands for war." (Ps. 18:34)

- "The LORD of Hosts is with us." (Ps. 46:7)

For Israel, God as Warrior was not scary — it was comforting. For any of us, as long as we are walking upright, it should be comforting, as well.

The prophets show God's final warrior victory. In Isaiah, Jeremiah, Ezekiel, Joel, Micah, and Zechariah, God's warrior role expands from national battles to cosmic end-time war. He defeats evil nations, rebellious kings, spiritual powers, and the forces of chaos. This crescendos in passages like, Isaiah 63:1–6 (God alone treads the winepress), and in Zechariah 14 (God fights for Jerusalem).

The Divine Warrior motif ultimately points to Messiah The OT warrior-God lays the groundwork for understanding. Messiah as the anointed warrior-king. Jesus ultimately defeats Satan (spiritual warfare). Christ wins ultimate victory over all powers.

Then the Old Testament warrior lands fully in the New Testament. The Old Testament presents God as the Divine Warrior who fights for His people, judges the wicked, overthrows spiritual and earthly enemies, and establishes His rule through power, strategy, and covenant faithfulness. This theme points directly to the Messiah, so we don't miss Him.

THE SILENCE BEFORE THE STORM

The Final Pause Before Christ Steps Into His Mission

Heaven has already chosen the moment. The Word has already become flesh. The Son has already entered the world He created. The eternal Christ is now living as Jesus of Nazareth— and yet… for thirty years the earth is quiet. No thunder. No miracles. No sermons. No disciples. No confrontations. No public declaration.

Just the Christ of God walking among humanity without revealing who He is. The universe is holding its breath. Because what is coming is not gentle, not small, not soft. What is coming is the boldest public ministry in human history. But first— the silence.

Christ waits for the Voice from Heaven. He is already the Son of God. Already the Lamb. Already the King. Already the Messiah. Already the Christ. But He waits for the Father's declaration. Christ does not begin His ministry based on potential, talent, or desire. He begins it based on timing. If Christ waited for the Voice of the Father, how much more should we? The hidden years teach us that divine purpose always matures in divine timing.

Heaven is loaded. Earth is quiet. While Christ grows in Wisdom and stature... Hell trembles. Angels watch. Prophets' words hang in the air. Creation groans, Israel sleeps. Rome tightens its grip. The Pharisees fortify their traditions. Demons choke the land. The oppressed cry out. Kingdoms rise and fall. Everything is building toward a moment. that will change history. Christ is not waiting idly. He is waiting strategically. Heaven does nothing prematurely.

The Christ of God is fully ready — but he respects the sequence. before He will overturn tables, confront Pharisees, cast out demons, cleanse lepers, call disciples, silence storms, feed multitudes, heal the broken, rebuke darkness, raise the dead. He must first be baptized, be affirmed, be anointed, be launched by the Father and the

Spirit. Christ honors the divine order He Himself established.

This is the final test of His humility and obedience.

The Final Days in Nazareth, Before the Jordan River, before John the Baptist's cry, before the heavens open… Christ lives His last days of anonymity. He completes His final tasks. He lays down His tools. He closes the door of the workshop. He leaves the streets He walked for decades. He walks away from the home that sheltered Him. He steps out of the ordinary and into destiny.

Imagine Nazareth on that last morning. No one realizes the Son of God is leaving. No one knows that history is shifting. No one sees that the Lamb is walking toward His mission. The Christ of God walks out quietly— because His entrance into public ministry will not be quiet at all.

The stage is set. John the Baptist is already crying in the wilderness "Prepare the way of the Lord." Demons sense movement and grow restless. Heaven is poised. The Father awaits His moment to speak. The Spirit is ready to descend. The Jordan River flows— waiting to cradle the body of the Son. Everything is aligned. The silence is about to break.

When Christ emerges from the hidden years He will shatter religious systems. He will dismantle demonic structures. He will confront corruption. He will expose hypocrisy. He will redefine righteousness. He will proclaim the kingdom. He will challenge Rome without lifting a sword. He will walk into every place that is broken. He will carry divine authority into human chaos. He will become the most misunderstood, most loved, most hated, most unstoppable Man on Earth. Volume I ends here because the next thing Christ does is step into the Jordan— and nothing will ever be the same again.

He has arrived. He has grown. He has waited. He has hidden. He has taken on flesh. He has submitted Himself to human life. He has honored the divine timetable.

And now— The Christ of God is about to be revealed. Volume II begins when the silence breaks. When He walks to the Jordan. When the heavens open. When the voice declares "THIS IS MY BELOVED SON." When the Lion of Judah begins His public roar.

EPILOGUE

Before The Heavens Open

The Christ of God has stepped into time. Eternity has wrapped itself in flesh. Heaven has entered Earth not with trumpets, but with footsteps in the dust of Nazareth. Every chapter of this volume has traced the quiet thunder of His eternal identity The Word who was with God and *was* God. The Son who walked in Eden. The Captain who met Joshua with drawn sword. The Fourth Man in the furnace, the One in Daniel's visions who receives everlasting dominion. The Lamb, **chosen** before the foundation of the world. The Child formed by the Spirit in Mary's womb. The Man maturing in silence, waiting for His hour. All of time bends toward Him. All of Scripture testifies of Him. All Creation anticipates Him.

And now, the world is standing on the threshold of His unveiling. The next sound we hear will be water, the Jordan River breaking around His body. The next voice we hear will be the Father, **"This is My beloved Son."** The next manifestation will be the Spirit descending like a dove. The silence is ending, the storm, beginning. The Christ of God is about to step into the spotlight to confront everything that is broken. You have seen Him eternal. You have seen Him pre-incarnate. You have seen Him hidden. Now prepare to see Him revealed. Volume II begins with the heavens opening.

CLOSING PRAYER

Lord Jesus Christ,
Eternal Word,
Son of the Living God—

As we close this volume,
we bow in awe before the mystery of Your glory.

You were before all things,
and by You all things exist.

You walked with Adam.
You wrestled with Jacob.
You stood with the faithful in fire.
You commanded the armies of Heaven.
You received dominion from the Ancient of Days.
You stepped into a womb
and became flesh for our salvation.

And You walked among us
with humility so deep
that most did not recognize You.

But we recognize You here.
We honor You.
We worship You.
We bow before You.

As we move toward the next volume,
open our eyes to the Christ of the Gospels—
the bold One, the fearless One,
the confrontational, compassionate, unstoppable One.

Let the revelation of who You were
before Bethlehem
prepare our hearts for who You will be
in Galilee, Jerusalem, and beyond.

Make us ready for Your voice.
Make us receptive to Your fire.
Make us unafraid to follow You
wherever Your footsteps lead.

You are the Alpha and the Omega.
The First and the Last.
The One who was, and is, and is to come.
We worship You, Christ of God.
In the Name of Jesus.

Amen.

CLOSING REFLECTION

Take a moment to sit with the enormity of what you've just explored. The Jesus of the Gospels is not a man who suddenly appears in Matthew 3. He is the Christ who existed before atoms, before angels, before time. He is not a figure who grew into divinity; He is divinity who wrapped Himself in humanity.

He is not simply a teacher; He is the Creator who became teachable. He did not arrive on Earth confused about His identity; He arrived with a mission older than the universe. And yet... He waited. He grew. He remained hidden. Because God's greatest works often unfold in secrecy before they explode into the world with force. As you turn from this volume to the next, consider this: The Christ who overturned tables is the same Christ who quietly planed wood in Nazareth. The Christ who rebuked storms is the same Christ who slept under them as a child. The Christ who commanded demons is the same Christ who learned the rhythms of human life.

Everything He will do publicly has already been shaped privately. And now— you are ready to walk with Him into His mission, His confrontation, His boldness, His brilliance, His fire. Volume II awaits you. And the Christ of God is walking toward the Jordan.

This book, <u>The Christ of GOD</u> is Volume I of a three-volume series. The images on any of the covers of this series are representative only. They are not to be inferred as images of Jesus Christ and are for teaching purposes only. Neither are these images to be worshipped.

Dr. Marlene Miles

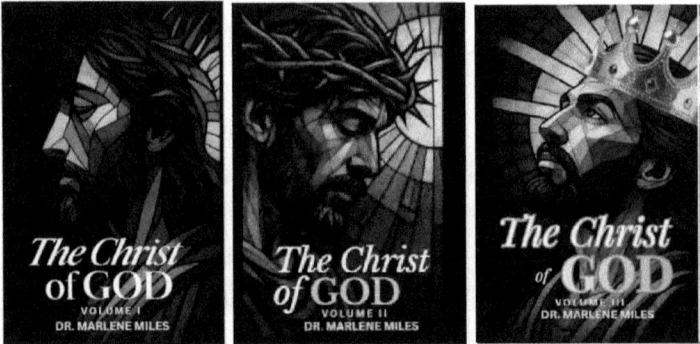

Dear Reader

May the Christ of God make Himself known to you—not as a distant figure of history, nor as a name shaped by tradition alone, but as the eternal Son who sees, governs, and keeps you. May your understanding be enlarged without pride, your reverence deepened without fear, and your faith steadied by Truth rather than emotion. As you close this volume, may what has been revealed here order your thinking, excite your spirit, and prepare you for the weight of what follows—knowing that the same Christ who is eternal is also faithful to finish what He begins.

Shalom,

Dr. Marlene Miles

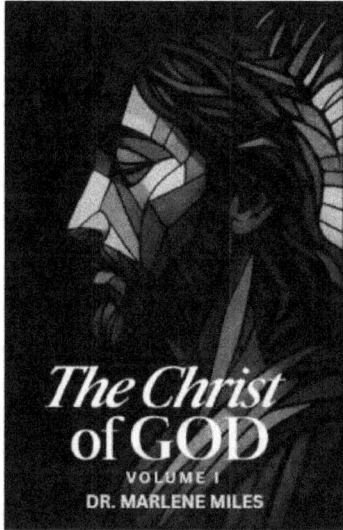

Prayerbooks by this author

There are some books that are only prayers. You just open up the book and pray.

Prayers Against Barrenness: *For Success in Business and Life*

Fruit of the Womb: *Prayers Against Barrenness*

Beauty Curses, *Warfare Prayers Against*
https://a.co/d/5Xlc20M

Courts of Marriage: Prayers for Marriage in the Courts of Heaven *(prayerbook)* https://a.co/d/cNAdgAq

Courtroom Warfare @ Midnight *(prayerbook)* https://a.co/d/5fc7Qdp

Demonic Cobwebs *(prayerbook)* https://a.co/d/fp9Oa2H

Every Evil Bird https://a.co/d/hF1kh1O

Gates of Thanksgiving

Spirits of Death, Hell & the Grave, Pass Over Me and My House

Throne of Grace: Courtroom Prayer

Warfare Prayer Against Poverty https://a.co/d/bZ611Yu

Other books by this author

Abundance of Jesus (The) https://a.co/d/5gHJVed

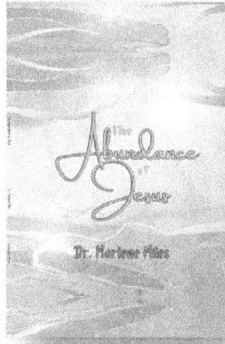

AK: The Adventures of the Agape Kid

Already Married in the Spirit: *Why You May Not Be Married in the Natural*

AMONG SOME THIEVES https://a.co/d/dkYT4ZV

Ancestral Powers

Anti-Marriage, *The Spirit of*

Backstabbers https://a.co/d/gi8iBxf

Barrenness, *Prayers Against* https://a.co/d/feUltIs

Battlefield of Marriage, *The*

Beware of the Dog: Prayers Against Dogs in the Dream.

Bless Your Food: *Let the Dining Table be Undefiled* *https://a.co/d/6oPMRDv*

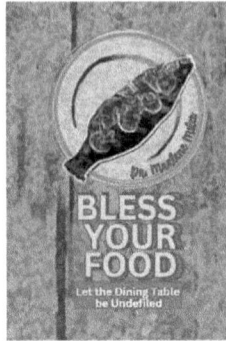

Blindsided: *Has the Old Man Bewitched You?*
https://a.co/d/5O2fLLR

Break Free from Collective Captivity

Broken Spirits & Dry Bones

By Means of a Whorish Father

Caged Life: Get Out Alive! https://a.co/d/bwPbksX

Casting Down Imaginations

Churchzilla, The Wanna-Be, Supposed-to-be Bride of Christ https://a.co/d/eAf5j3x

Collateral Damage: *When What Happened Spiritually Was Your Fault*

Demonic Cobwebs (prayerbook)

Demonic Time Bombs

Demons Hate Questions

Devil Loves Trauma, *The*

Devil Weapons: Unforgiveness, Bitterness,...

The Devourers: Thieves of Darkness 2

Do Not Swear by the Moon

Don't Refuse Me, Lord (4 book series)
https://a.co/d/idP34LG

Dream Defilement

The Emptiers: *Thieves of Darkness, 1*
https://a.co/d/5I4n5mc

Evil Touch

Failed Assignment

Fantasy Spirit Spouse https://a.co/d/hW7oYbX

FAT Demons (The): *Breaking Demonic Curses*
https://a.co/d/4kP8wV1

The Fold (5-book series)

- The Fold (Book 1)
- Name Your Seed (Book 2)
- The Poor Attitudes of Money (3)
- Do Not Orphan Your Seed (4)
- For the Sake of the Gospel (5)
- My Sowing Journal

Gang Ups: Touch Not God's Anointed

Gathered: No Longer Scattered
https://a.co/d/1i5DPIX

Getting Rid of Evil Spiritual Food

https://a.co/d/i2L3WYQ

got HEALING? Verses for Life

got LOVE? Verses for Life https://a.co/d/8seXHPd

got HOPE? Verses for Life

got money? https://a.co/d/g2av41N

Has My Soul Been Sold? https://a.co/d/dyB8hhA

Here Come the Horns: *Skilled to Destroy*
https://a.co/d/cZiNnkP

Hidden Sins: Hidden Iniquity

https://a.co/d/4Mth0wa

How to Dental Assist

How to Dental Assist2: Be Productive, Not Wasteful

How to STOP Being a Blind Witch or Warlock

I Take It Back

Irresistible: Jesus' Triumphal Entry
https://a.co/d/d09IfEC

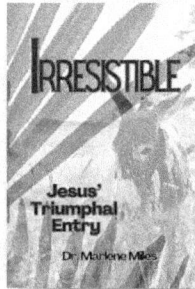

Legacy

Let Me Have A Dollar's Worth
https://a.co/d/h8F8XgE

Level the Playing Field

Living for the NOW of God

Lose My Location https://a.co/d/crD6mV9

Love Breaks Your Heart

Made Perfect In Love

Mammon https://a.co/d/29yhMG7

Man Safari, *The*

Marriage Ed. Rules of Engagement & Marriage

Made Perfect in Love

Money Hunters: Beware of Those

Money on the Altar https://a.co/d/4EqJ2Nr

Mulberry Tree, *The* https://a.co/d/9nR9rRb

Motherboard (The)~ *Soul Prosperity Series*

Name Your Seed

Occupy: *Until I Return* https://a.co/d/bZ7ztUy

Plantation Souls

Players Gonna Play

Portals: Shut the Front Door: Prayers to Close Evil Portals.

Power Money: Nine Times the Tithe

https://a.co/d/gRt41gy

The Power to Get Wealth https://a.co/d/e4ub4Ov

Powers Above

The Robe, Part 1, The Lessons of Joseph

The Robe, Part II, The Lessons of Joseph

Seasons of Grief

Seasons of Waiting

Seasons of War

Second Marriage, Third~~, *Any Marriage*
https://a.co/d/6m6GN4N

Seducing Spirits: Idolatry & Whoredoms

https://a.co/d/4Jq4WEs

Shut the Front Door: *Prayers to Close Portals*
https://a.co/d/cH4TWJj

Sift You Like Wheat

Six Men Short: What Has Happened to all the Men?

SLAVE

Sleep Afflictions & Really Bad Dreams
https://a.co/d/f8sDmgv

Soul Prosperity soul prosperity series 3

https://a.co/d/5p8YvCN

Souls Captivity soul prosperity series 2

The Spirit of Anti-Marriage

The Spirit of Poverty https://a.co/d/abV2o2e

Spiritual Thieves https://a.co/d/eqPPz33

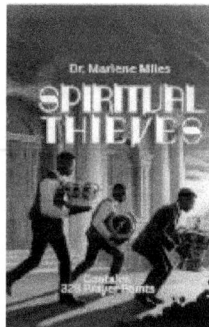

StarStruck- Triangular Power series.

SUNBLOCK- Triangular Power series.

The Swallowers: *Thieves of Darkness*, 3

Take It Back

This Is NOT That: How to Keep Demons from Coming at You

Time Is of the Essence

Too Many Wives: *Why You Have Lady Problems*

Tormenting Spirits   https://a.co/d/dAogEJf

Toxic Souls

Triangular Power *(series),* Powers Above, SUNBLOCK, Do Not Swear by the Moon, STARSTRUCK

Unbreak My Heart: *Don't Let Me Die*

Uncontested Doom

Unguarded Hours, *The*

Unseen Life, *The* (forthcoming)

Upgrade: How to Get Out of Survival Mode Toxic Souls (Book 2 of series) , Legacy (Book 3 of series)

The Wasters: *Thieves of Darkness,* Bk 2
https://a.co/d/bUvI9Jo

What Have You to Declare? What Do You Have With You from Where You've Been?

When I Was A Child, *I Prayed As a Child*

When the Devourer is Rebuked

https://a.co/d/1HVv8oq

WTH? Get Me Out of This Hell
https://a.co/d/a7WBGJh

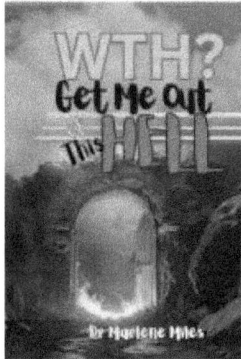

The Wilderness Romance *(series)* This series is about conducting a Godly relationship and marriage with someone who is a Wilderness person. It is about how to recognize it and navigate through it. These books are about how not to get caught up in such.

- *The Social Wilderness*
- *The Sexual Wilderness*
- *The Spiritual Wilderness*

Other Series

The Fold (a series on Godly finances) https://a.co/d/4hz3unj

Soul Prosperity Series https://a.co/d/bz2M42q

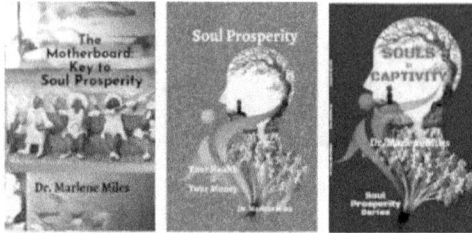

Spirit Spouse books

https://a.co/d/9VehDSo

https://a.co/d/97sKOwm

Battlefield of Marriage, The

https://a.co/d/eUDzizO

Players Gonna Play

https://a.co/d/2hzGw3N

Sent Spirit Spouse (can someone send you a spirit spouse? This book is not yet released.)

Matters of the Heart, Made Perfect in Love

https://a.co/d/70MQW3O , Love Breaks Your Heart
https://a.co/d/4KvuQLZ, Unbreak My Heart
https://a.co/d/84ceZ6M Broken Spirits & Dry Bones
https://a.co/d/e6iedNP

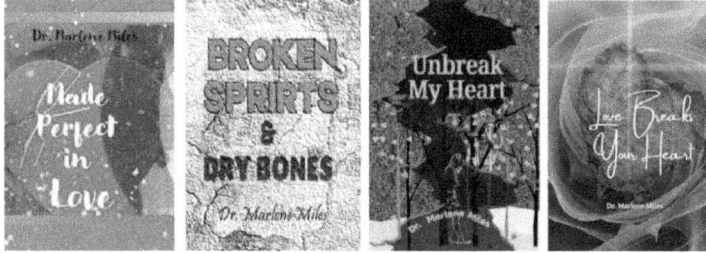

Thieves of Darkness series

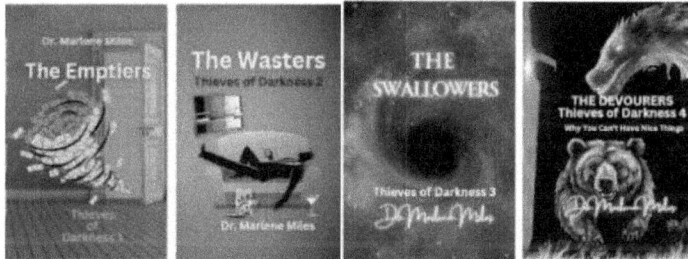

The Emptiers https://a.co/d/heio0dO

The Wasters https://a.co/d/5TG1iNQ

The Swallowers https://a.co/d/1jWhM6G

The Devourers: Why We Can't Have Nice Things
https://a.co/d/87Tejbf

Spiritual Thieves

Triangular Powers https://a.co/d/aUCjAWC

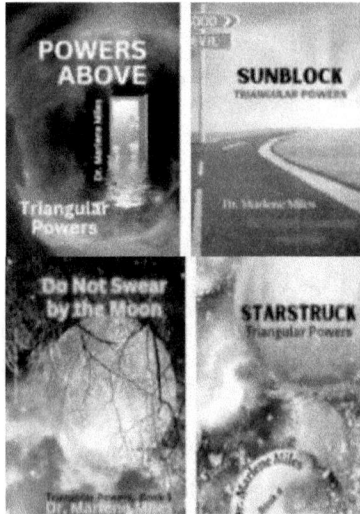

Upgrade (series) *How to Get Out of Survival Mode*
https://a.co/d/aTERhX0

www.ingramcontent.com/pod-product-compliance
Lightning Source LLC
LaVergne TN
LVHW052028080426
835513LV00018B/2228